D1544882

Praise for
Same Words, Different Language

"Barbara Annis is a pioneer in encouraging the world of business to understand the differences between the way men and women communicate. She stands apart as an intelligent advisor to corporations, teaching them how to meld the talents of men and women into an effective whole. *Same Words, Different Language* is necessary reading for every person who wants to be better understood and be more understanding."

—**Marianne J. Legato,** M.D., F.A.C.P, Professor of Clinical Medicine, Columbia University, Founder, Foundation for Gender-Specific Medicine, Inc.

"*Same Words, Different Language* remains a landmark work that examines today's workplace opportunities and challenges through a social interaction lens. It demonstrates why gender intelligence will inspire a culture of inclusiveness and create a sustainable source of economic advantage for individuals, leaders, and their organizations."

—**Lara Warner,** Chief Financial Officer, Credit Suisse Investment Bank

"Gender diversity centers on creating an inclusive culture for everyone, one that views and values people, first and foremost, for their potential to make a positive contribution. I strongly believe that when we better understand each other, we better understand our customers and that's a tremendous competitive advantage. In a world where smart communication and even smarter listening is a business imperative, *Same Words, Different Language* is the guidebook to that advantage."

—**Anka Wittenberg,** Chief Diversity and Inclusion Officer, SAP

"The problem isn't the differences between men and women, but how we recognize, value, and leverage those differences. Gender intelligence comes from understanding and appreciating the unique talents and skills that men and women bring to the table, and how their natural complement can improve productivity, innovativeness, and economic growth."

—**Janet C. Salazar,** CEO and Founder, IMPACT Leadership 21

"Annis confronts, head on, the elephant in the room. Men and women are not the same, are quite different, and actually complement each other perfectly. It's about time we begin to understand, appreciate, and value each other's ways of thinking and acting. *Same Words, Different Language* bravely illuminates the path to greater understanding."

—**Jane Allen,** Chief Diversity Officer, Deloitte Canada

"Same Words, Different Language helps illuminate the communications differences that exist between women and men. These differences can get in the way of teamwork and performance. Given that our management ranks are almost evenly split between women and men, understanding these differences in order to facilitate better interaction and communications will truly help us succeed."

—**Philip Marineau,** CEO, Levi Strauss & Company

"As a practitioner toiling diligently in the arena of gender awareness, executive coaching, and personal transformation, Barbara Annis is a living legend. She has been a locomotive for change in the corporate world for almost 30 years. In that time, she's pulled desired changes out of over 50,000 business executives and professionals in over 8,000 workshop seminars…. She unleashes the energies we need to envision and deliver futures we've only vaguely dreamed. And she does it by empowering teams of men and women to work in transformative partnerships, in collaborations that turn gender differences from a liability to an engine of new abilities."

—**O. Woodward Buckner,** Chief Executive Officer, Buckner & Co.

"Same Words, Different Language makes sense of the neurological differences between the genders. It builds a new form of conversation between men and women. More importantly, it builds a new form of collaboration. For over 2.5 million years, men and women have worked together to accomplish unreasonable outcomes during unreasonable times. But they've barely begun to tap the powers of their synergy. *Same Words, Different Language* is a seminal contribution to this new level of inquiry."

—**Howard Bloom,** Author, *Global Brain*

"There is a new frontier awaiting us, one that's made itself clear in Annis's adventures on the often stormy front-lines of diversity, relationship, and gender-awareness management. *Same Words, Different Language* is the outcome of 3,600,000,000 man/woman hours of live transformational interactive experiences. I suspect cultural anthropologists, semanticists, neuroscientists, psychosocial biologists, strategists, organizational behaviorists and talk-show hosts will be 'plumbing the gold' from this practitioner's treasure mine of real-world experiences for many years to come."

—**Chief Commentator,** Business News-CNBC, Former Chairman of the FDIC and RTC

"Thank you, thank you. I always thought that men were the ones who needed to understand; little did I know that I had a lot to learn about my own misinterpretations. I am so relieved that I can actually be a woman at work instead of a man in women's clothes."

—**Cathy Diamond,** IBM Executive

"I didn't know what to expect, and being a man, I was very careful on the first day. What a positive surprise! I actually enjoyed every single minute, while learning more than I have in any course. This was a watershed moment for all of us."

—Deputy Minister, UK Treasury Department

"No one better than Barbara Annis can show you how to build a high-performing culture of inclusion. Years of extensive research and practical experience have given Barbara a unique perspective on how to overcome the deeply entrenched obstacles that create invisible chasms in organizations. Her incisive views on how men and women can most effectively work together will guide you in developing a leadership context where all differences can become complementary strengths."

—Hubert Saint-Onge, Chief Executive Officer, Author, *Leveraging Communities of Practice for Strategic Advance*

Same Words, Different Language

Same Words, Different Language

A Proven Guide for Creating Gender Intelligence at Work

Third Edition

Barbara Annis

Associate Editor: Kim Boedigheimer
Senior Marketing Manager: Stephane Nakib
Cover Designer: Chuti Prasertsith
Managing Editor: Sandra Schroder
Senior Project Editor: Lori Lyons
Project Manager: Maureen Forys
Copy Editor: Rebecca Rider
Proofreader: Rebecca Rider
Indexer: Valerie Perry
Compositor: Maureen Forys

© 2016 by Pearson Education, Inc.
Old Tappan, New Jersey 07675

For information about buying this title in bulk quantities, or for special sales opportunities (which may include electronic versions; custom cover designs; and content particular to your business, training goals, marketing focus, or branding interests), please contact our corporate sales department at corpsales@pearsoned.com or (800) 382-3419.

For government sales inquiries, please contact governmentsales@pearsoned.com.

For questions about sales outside the U.S., please contact intlcs@pearson.com.

Company and product names mentioned herein are the trademarks or registered trademarks of their respective owners.

All rights reserved. Printed in the United States of America. This publication is protected by copyright, and permission must be obtained from the publisher prior to any prohibited reproduction, storage in a retrieval system, or transmission in any form or by any means, electronic, mechanical, photocopying, recording, or likewise. For information regarding permissions, request forms, and the appropriate contacts within the Pearson Education Global Rights & Permissions Department, please visit www.pearsoned.com/permissions/.

1   16

ISBN-10: 0-13-451327-4
ISBN-13: 978-0-13-451327-0

Pearson Education LTD.
Pearson Education Australia PTY, Limited
Pearson Education Singapore, Pte. Ltd.
Pearson Education Asia, Ltd.
Pearson Education Canada, Ltd.
Pearson Educación de Mexico, S.A. de C.V.
Pearson Education—Japan
Pearson Education Malaysia, Pte. Ltd.

Library of Congress Control Number: 2016935637

To my partner and husband, Paul Reed Currie, whose amazing support, love, and extraordinary integrity I always admire and treasure.

And to my wonderful children, Lauren, Sasha, Stephane, and Christian; my bonus children, Zachary, Kelly, and Jeremy; and my grandchildren, Grayson, Riley, Brydan, Jake, Alaia, Cameron, and Colin.

Contents at Glance

Contents

Acknowledgments

Thank you to the many thousands of men and women around the world who have participated in this work and who have ensured that it made a lasting difference. Thank you to Susanna Margolis, who carefully crafted the language and made this book sing. Thank you to the teams at Happenstance and Pearson and to our literary agent, Carol Mann, for bringing this work into the world. I also want to acknowledge our friends, colleagues, and clients for having made tremendous contributions in their sphere of influence.

I wish to thank Lee Akazaki, Kenchiro Akiyama, Jane Allen, Jennifer Allyn, Shahla Aly, Heidi Rottbol Andersen, Greg Van Asperen, Beth Axelrod, Robin Baliszewski, Clare Beckton, Jim Beqaj, Jill Beresford, Megan Beyer, Gina Bianchini, Johan Bjorklund, Rob Bloom, Maryann Bloomfield, Dr. Iris Bohnet, Lynda Bowles, Stephanie Hanbury Brown, Woody Buckner, Victoria Budson, James Bush, Dr. Larry Cahill, Bob Cancalosi, Susan Cartsonis, Kenneth Chenault, Jennifer Christie, Adel Cotichini, Kevin Cox, Judy Dahm, Geena Davis, Christa Dowling, Nancy Elder, Carol Evans, John Fallon, John Fayad, Dr. Helen Fisher, Stacey Fisher, Nancy Forsyth, Gaby Giglio, Ed Gilligan, Dr. John Gray, Neena Gupta, Dr. Ruben Gur, Bruce Haase, Nadine Hack, John Hart, Jane Hewson, Jan Hill, Arianna Huffington, Swanee Hunt, Theresa Jabour, Dr. Joseph Jaworski, Elisabeth Jensen, Gail Kelman, Robin Kennedy, Mary Jo Kovach, Michael Kubina, Sonya Kunkel, Dr. George Labovitz, Stan Labovitz, Jennifer Laidlaw, Uno Langmann, Carolyn Lawrence, Bruce Leamon, Chuck Ledsinger, Dr. Marianne Legato, Maria LeRose, Elizabeth Lesser, Pernille Spiers-Lopez, Renee Lundholm, Anne Madison, Susanna Margolis, Marguerite McLeod, Ramón Martín, Graciela Meibar, Kathleen Merron, Dr. Keith Merron, Pat Mitchell, Dr. Anne Moir, Betsy Myers, Richard Nesbitt, Kenna Ose, Constance

Peak, Paola Corna Pellegrini, Kerrie Peraino, Matt Peterson, Phyllis Stewart Pires, Allison Pogemiller, Jennifer Reynolds, Dr. Alan Richter, Adel Rickets, Eiko Saito, Janet Salazar, Hubert Saint-Onge, Ulla Sanbaek, Sheryl Sandberg, Nicole Schwab, Maria Shriver, Dr. Janet Smith, Jim Hagerman Snabe, Val Sorbie, Erin Stein, Sean Stowers, Claudia Studle, Kate Sweetman, Dr. Deborah Tannen, Kendra Thomas, Rachel Thomas, Aniela Unguresan, Dr. Karin Verland, Dr. Elena Vigna, Emily Viner, Lara Warner, James Ward, Gillian Whitebread, Donna Wilson, Marie Wilson, Oprah Winfrey, Dr. Sandra Witelson, Anka Wittenberg, Dr. Jeannette Wolfe, Janet Wood, and Jacki Zehner.

To all the amazing deeply committed women and men leaders and staff at the Women's Leadership Board, Harvard Kennedy School, and to the Edge Certified Foundation; I am honored to partner with you in creating a world where men and women are equally valued and respected in all aspects of economic, political, and social life. To the Clinton Global Initiative for bringing gender intelligence to its global efforts to create and implement innovative solutions for the world's most pressing challenges; to the remarkable board members of the Institute for Women's Studies in the Arab World (IWSAW) at Lebanese American University, in Beirut, Lebanon, for their enduring contribution to empowering women in the Arab world through development, programs, and education; and to all the organizations and their men and women who are embracing gender intelligence because they want to work and succeed together including:

American Express, Ashridge Business School, Baker Tilly Virchow Krause, Bank of America, Bentley University, Blake, Cassels & Graydon, BMO Financial Group, Choice Hotels International, CIBC, Costco, Crayola, Credit Suisse, Danish CEO Network, Dassault Systèmes, Deloitte, Deutsche Bank, Disney, eBay, EDS, Electrolux, Ericsson, Federal Business Development Bank, Fidelity Investments, Financial Times, Ford Motor Company, Fordham University, Gender Equality Project Geneva, Goodman & Carr, Google, Greenberg Traurig, Guardian Life Insurance Company of America, Harvard University, HSBC Bank, IBM, IKEA, Imperial Oil, Industry Canada, Kellogg's, KVINFO, Johnson & Johnson, LEGO, Levi Strauss & Company, Loblaws, Mattel, McDonalds, Microsoft, Molson Coors, Motorola, Department of National Defense Canada, Nav Canada,

Nissan, Novartis, Oliver Wyman, Pax World, Pearson Education, Pfizer, Prentice Hall, PricewaterhouseCoopers, RBC Financial, Ritchie Bros. Auctioneers, SAP, Scotiabank, SMBC, Sun Life Insurance, Swedish-American Chamber of Commerce, Symcor, Tambrands, Technip, Toshiba, Treasury Board of Canadian Secretariat, UBS Investments, Unilever, U.S. Chamber of Commerce, U.S. Department of Justice, U.S. Department of Defense, Wells Fargo, Wells Fargo Women of Influence, Women in Film, Wood Gundy Securities, and Xerox.

About the Author

Barbara Annis, a world-renowned expert on inclusive leadership, corporate culture, and gender issues, is the founder and CEO of Gender Intelligence Group (formerly Barbara Annis & Associates), which advocates for gender intelligence in Fortune 500 companies and global organizations. Her work has pioneered a transformational shift in how to leverage gender differences to achieve organizational success.

Annis began her career as the first woman in sales at Sony, where she achieved 14 Outstanding Sales Achievement Awards and Sony's MVP Award. Since founding the Gender Intelligence Group, her global team of associates has facilitated more than 8,000 corporate workshops and conducted thousands of leadership assessments and executive coaching sessions. Based on Annis's breakthrough research on the practice and benefits of inclusive leadership and gender diversity, Gender Intelligence Group today offers diagnostics, workshops, and coaching both onsite and online.

Annis is also the chairperson emerita of the Women's Leadership Board at Harvard Kennedy School and the author of *Gender Intelligence, Breakthrough Strategies for Increasing Diversity and Improving Your Bottom Line,* coauthored with Dr. Keith Merron; *Leadership and the Sexes,* coauthored with Michael Gurian; and *Work with Me,* cowritten with John Gray.

Introduction

In the nearly 15 years since the first edition of this book, much progress has been made toward a more balanced gender distribution in corporate organizations. The number of women in positions of responsibility and leadership has risen dramatically in business, the professions, and government. Why, therefore, is a third edition of *Same Words, Different Language* so necessary?

Because the numbers, while gratifying, aren't the point. After all, you can have an army a million strong, but if you send it into battle unarmed, your chances of achieving victory are minimal. Similarly, adding women to the ranks of organizations only throws into sharp relief what the women, the men they work beside, and above all, the organizations they work for are missing out on—and what all will continue to miss out on so long as women and men mouth the same words but speak a different language from one another.

Here's the issue: the science is now pretty clear that men and women go about the process of thinking, looking at the world, and navigating their way through it in gender-specific ways. The differences are not solely the result of a particular culture's socialization; they are, in fact, hard-wired variations in brain structure and biochemistry. Women in corporate life are plunked down in a cultural construct that has been defined for generations by male behavior and male-specific rules, and the way to succeed in such a situation is to adopt that behavior and bend to those rules. In doing so, however, women leave at the door their natural way of looking at the world and their natural habits of perception, problem solving, and collaboration. And like the hapless soldier in the thick of battle without a weapon, they feel frustrated—shortchanged. Worse, their organizations are shortchanged; they are losing out not just on the unique benefits that women's gender-specific attributes can bring, but more to the point, they are missing out on the exceptional advantage that can be produced when both women and men understand the gender differences and know how to optimize them. When that happens, when men and women are finally speaking the same language and can take from and add to the other's gender-specific strengths and abilities, the work they produce together, not surprisingly, is far better than anything either gender could manage on its own.

For more than a quarter of a century, I have been involved in the effort to get women and men to speak the same language and to work together with gender intelligence—that is, with an understanding of and appreciation for the natural differences between men and women.[1] I've held countless workshops all over the world, have consulted with thousands of corporate leaders, and have created an online curriculum, "Be Gender Intelligent," to carry the message to as many people as possible. The results have been gratifying beyond my expectations. The reason is simple: being gender intelligent works. The organization functions better, the people who work there are more engaged, and the performance results are off the charts.

That's what this edition of *Same Words, Different Language* is about. It's your guide to becoming gender intelligent and to infusing gender intelligence into your workplace. Updated to reflect the lessons learned from that quarter century of experience, it will help you learn proactively how to be gender intelligent in ways that beneficially impact how you manage a team, problem-solve, think innovatively, coach, counsel, advise, and execute. (I don't mean just at work, either; the lessons here will work anywhere women and men come into contact with one another.)

Be prepared to see and hear yourself in many of the scenarios in these pages. Are you pretty sure you're free of preexisting ideas— and certainly of prejudices—about the other gender? Don't be surprised—and don't be angry with yourself—to find it isn't so. Face what you find honestly—and expect the same from the woman or man sitting across the table from you.

---

1. Gender Intelligence® is a registered trademark of the Gender Intelligence Group.

Then get ready to peer inside the mind of the other gender. You may realize that you have very probably misinterpreted the behavior of others in the past. You may find that your own gender-related behavior sometimes stymies the very goals you think you're pursuing. You'll certainly see just how different are the realities the two genders see, and how the same words can mean to the other gender almost the opposite of what you think they mean.

All this can help you listen differently, avoid misunderstanding, and get your own message across in a way that the person you're communicating with will understand.

It won't take long for you to see that although men and women are certainly different, there's a lot more uniting than dividing us. We all want the same things from our work: the feeling that we are contributing something of value, the opportunity as individuals to learn and grow, and the chance to be part of an organization that makes both those goals possible.

—Barbara Annis

Please visit www.pearsoned.com/gender-intelligence for information about our online transformational learning experience.

1

It's Time to Change the Water We Swim In

Water to the fish, air to the bird, both can't see it, but they can feel the turbulent forces of change.

—Stephen Covey, *The 7 Habits of Highly Effective People*

The first time I talked to them, they told me theirs was the kind of New York law firm that young lawyers were "dying" to work for. But from what other people had told me about the place, I suspected people were "dying" from working there. I was right. In the last year, several of their top lawyers, all women, had left. The women said they left for "family reasons" or "work-life balance." I knew there was more to it than that.

It really was an impressive law firm. The office was huge and luxurious, and the client list was a Who's Who of top companies. Working there was every young lawyer's dream. The partners at the firm wanted the best talent at any price and had no problem attracting the cream of the crop of law school graduates.

Yet something was going wrong. In addition to the loss of several top female lawyers, a number of talented younger lawyers, male and female but predominantly female, had also recently left. There was a trend here, as one of the firm's clients noticed. The client, a bank I worked for, gave the law firm my number. "You people need help," the banker told the firm's partners.

When I started meeting senior partners and employees at the firm, I saw the problems right away. Both men and women at the firm complained about the working environment. One younger partner told me that the senior partners regularly made inappropriate comments about women. Several people mentioned the women partners who had left the previous year. "Oh yeah, there was that long-legged girl who was working for us," recalled one of the senior partners, conjuring up what seemed to be an already indistinct memory of one of those women; he thought she'd left for family reasons. A junior partner told me about a dinner party where senior partners exchanged sexist jokes while the women at the table stared stonily, pretending not to hear, or rolled their eyes in the best good humor they could muster. That gave me a good idea of the kinds of problems they were probably having.

I decided to meet up with the "long-legged" ex-partner, whose name was Sandra. As it turned out, she hadn't left her job for "family reasons" at all. Shortly after she left, she launched her own firm. A single mother with a ten-year-old daughter, Sandra welcomed me into her stylish new office. A graduate of a prestigious law school, she had all the polish and assurance her credentials and experience suggested. Her new firm was doing lots of business, and professionally, she told me, she was a lot happier now.

Slowly, the story of why she had left her old job unfolded. Sandra had suspected it would be a tough place to work when she was hired. It was, but she stuck it out for 12 years. "I had genuine commitment to the firm and to the work I was doing," she told me. "But then it just got to be too much. I couldn't stand the atmosphere anymore. By the end, I had to drag myself to work." What was going on?

As Sandra put it, no matter how hard she worked and no matter how many hours she put in, she never felt like she was regarded as "one of the boys." At meetings, the partners would discuss business as if she weren't even there. "I didn't feel valued," Sandra said. "It got to the point where I had to admit that nothing was improving"—certainly not if a partner could still refer to this grown-up professional as a "girl"—and a "long-legged" one at that.

It was a shame, she said, because she loved working with her clients and found the atmosphere stimulating. That's what kept her going for so long, she said. She had thrived on the challenging client relationships, and she was aware that working with these clients had enabled her to hone her professional skills. But at some point it occurred to her that she worked in two worlds. Her clients treated her like a professional, and her colleagues continually treated her as though she were a subordinate. Sandra felt that no one valued her or recognized her unique skills, and since she wasn't being given the responsibilities she deserved, she simply decided to move on. As she put it, "What choice did I have?"

To avoid having to explain, she told her associates that she needed more time with her daughter. They were surprised, and they were sad to see her go, but they took her at her word. Everyone left it at that.

The Women's Side of the Story

I knew it wasn't that simple, and I knew it wasn't just Sandra's story. I arranged to meet up with six other women who had left the firm the previous year to hear what they had to say. Their complaints were almost exactly the same as Sandra's. They weren't treated as equal colleagues no matter how much they worked. Instead, they were constantly singled out; they felt they were viewed as being "less confident" than their male counterparts, but they weren't sure why. Every time they asked a rigorous question it was turned back onto them, as if the men thought the women were being suspicious rather than simply seeking information.

One woman complained to her associates that she was never given high-profile cases. "Women work on these cases, but we are never in the limelight," she said. In fact, the women felt they were shown even less respect than their junior male colleagues. Even the support staff gave a lot more "support" to men than to them. When I asked the women how their male colleagues reacted when they tried to talk about these issues, they responded, to a woman, that they were told "we were exaggerating or over-personalizing. They said we were being overly critical or making a mountain out of a molehill."

In the end, these women too felt unheard, under-challenged, and under-valued by their colleagues. They were paid less and got less respect than their male colleagues. But the worst of it, they all agreed, was the feeling of isolation they had felt working at this celebrated and highly respected firm. They weren't part of the "boys' network," but there was no "girls' network." They felt as if they were on their own, adrift in a sea of problems that couldn't be discussed with any-one else, let alone solved.

So like Sandra, they talked with their feet. And since the women were sure no one would understand their real reasons for leaving, they each gave the easiest, most legitimate excuse they could think of, usually a variation on the same theme. Several called it "work-life balance," a catch phrase for "family." The rest said they needed more "flexibility," a word which, to their lawyer partners, sounded like about the same thing.

The partners believed the women's excuses. Everyone took the women's words at face value. "Leaving for family reasons" had a familiar ring to it. As some of the partners told me themselves, "It goes with being a woman." It was predictable. None of them made the connection between the atmosphere they described to me and the women's departures. Seven lawyers out of the door in one year, all women, and no one saw a trend!

The Lights Start Going On

But there *was* a connection. My colleague Keith and I had interviewed almost everyone working for the firm, either individually or in focus groups. Many employees felt the firm's environment was dominated by patronizing behavior. Of course, a lot of women felt this way, but surprisingly, so did a lot of men. Many of the lawyers complained about a macho atmosphere, elitism on the part of senior partners, and a "star status" attributed to certain partners. They resented the turf wars and objected to the endless meetings, to which only certain partners were invited, while others emphatically were not. Many men confessed that they were uncomfortable with the environment at the firm, but that they were afraid to bring up their concerns with the senior partners. There was a lot of pressure on them to conform.

Needless to say, the partners were not too happy to hear the results of my interviews. True to their lawyerly training, they particularized or picked apart every complaint set before them. They demanded examples of patronizing behavior, and then dismissed those examples for one reason or another. They said things like, "Oh, it must have been so-and-so who said that. She has it in for me." I reported that one woman was tired of being told "not to worry her little head over things." The woman was, in fact, petite. "I know who that is," blurted out one partner. "She just has a short-person complex. That's got nothing to do with gender."

Their response to the complaints: kill the messenger. If I had left them to it, they would have spent the entire day dissecting each complaint to satisfy themselves that not one of them was legitimate. There were moments when I wished I could just leave them to their own nitpicking, but I pressed on, trying to steer through the acrimony until the senior partners saw what was going on.

After several hours of arguing, one of the women in the group decided to speak up, and the tone in the room changed. It was not beside the point that she was their top litigation lawyer, nor that she had been silent up to that moment. She looked at the senior partners and addressed them directly. "You regard me as if I were your daughter," she said. "You may not realize it, but that's what you do." It was, she told them, behavior she found humiliating.

Her words hit the mark. For a moment, there was silence; then the floodgates opened. "You mean, I do that?" one man asked. When the partners started to see how their own actions affected the women working at their firm, all the themes we had been discussing took on a new light. Until then, no one had actually made a connection between the departures of the seven women the previous year and the complaints others were making about the environment. The partners all saw them as "isolated" incidents. Then, all of a sudden, everyone saw the women's departures as part of a larger problem: the working atmosphere at the firm was corrosive. The atmosphere wasn't actually killing individual people, but it was quickly killing the firm.

It didn't take the partners long to see how much the bad atmosphere was costing them. Everyone knew that when the women left, they took valuable clients with them. Everyone was aware that losing those clients had cost the firm millions in lost business. When they calculated the total cost of seven lawyers leaving, it really sunk in.

"I guess we have a problem," one partner concluded.

"I think that's putting it mildly," said another.

It's tempting—and satisfying—to see this as a tale of a group of angry lawyers learning a lesson about the high price they paid for treating women badly. The male partners at the firm said and did things that were offensive to women. The women eventually threw in the towel and took business worth millions with them. Keith and I made the men aware of how they had caused the women's departure, and they resolved to change their ways. But how?

Solving the problem in this firm, as in most companies, is not about finding a villain, or deciding who's right and who's wrong. It's not about men "learning their lessons." It's about changing an environment that's hurting everyone. Law firms, banks, and large international accounting firms aren't the only places where corrosive work environments make people feel alienated and frustrated. I see these environments in all kinds of organizations and fields: sales, manufacturing, retail, education, and government.

The good news? Each of us can help change that environment, no matter where we work.

The situation in the law firm, like that in every company or organization I work for, is the result of misunderstandings. Those misunderstandings start because men and women differ in fundamental ways: in how we think, how we communicate, how we assimilate information, and more. When we don't understand those differences, we project our reactions onto the other gender and judge the gender as a whole, without ever understanding the real message or what an individual's behavior really means. Both men and women play an equal role in the misunderstandings.

And both men and women can change their behavior. It all starts with identifying the environment in which we spend our working lives, and in doing what we can to make it a place where we can all thrive.

The Fish Aquarium

If you only take one lesson from this book, it's this: men and women are different. I hope you'll forgive me if, for the sake of analogy, I use the concept of men and women as different (but both extraordinary) types of fish.

Think of today's work environment as an aquarium you own in which beautiful red fish have been flourishing for years. One day, you decide to add blue fish. If it worked for the red ones, it'll work for the blue ones, you tell yourself. They're both fish, after all. The only difference is their color. But when you add the blue fish, something goes wrong. They don't like it. They don't flourish. The water doesn't seem to suit them, and pretty soon they start to make the red fish unhappy, too. The conclusion is inescapable. If you want both fish to flourish, you have to change the water.

That's where the workplace is right now. There's something wrong with the water we're swimming in. Many women aren't happy at work, and neither are a lot of men. It's not women's fault. And it's not men's fault. It's the water we're swimming in.

Most companies that come to me for help think they have a "women problem." Either they've had a problem advancing women, or they're losing women and don't understand why. Sometimes companies call me because an inner group—usually women—has gathered and decided something needs to be done about how women are treated there.

Although most of the business leaders I meet know that there is a problem in today's workplace that needs to be addressed, many believe it's just a matter of "getting the numbers right." A manager from a major pharmaceutical company recently told me this: "Just look at the facts. The policies are there to ensure equality between women and men." A young investment banker attending one of my workshops said, "Our bank is proud of the progress we have made with our female staff. We even have two at the executive management level." Other companies I deal with boast about how their programs to promote women in management or through their special women's networks are "taking care of things." But nothing could be further from the truth.

That truth is that women are generally less comfortable in today's work environment than men. It's no mystery why. Despite the fact that today, women make up the majority of both university undergraduates, and top-position graduates in business, law, accounting, medicine, sociology, and education, and despite women's massive entry into most areas of employment, the working world they have joined was designed, for the most part, by men! It's nobody's *fault*. It's just that, generally speaking, when the corporate model was developed, the overwhelming majority of the workforce was male. As a result, men have written the basic rules for how almost everything

in the office gets done: from writing reports, to conducting evaluations, to the way board meetings are run. Those rules have stuck, even
though they don't reflect the way many individual men would now
choose to run things.

Traditional and New Business Models

The traditional business model is so common and so universal
that no one even notices it. It's invisible, like water is to the fish. Yet
it was essentially written from a mindset that makes sense to men: it's
based on a military model of command and control, one that is mirrored also in team sports. It looks roughly like this:

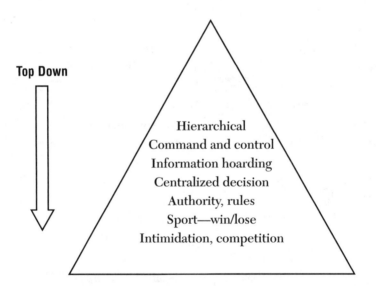

The Traditional Business Model

Why do women struggle with this model? It simply doesn't cor-
respond to the way they naturally think and work. If women were left
to their own devices, they would write a very different set of rules for
the business world. Women naturally seek collaboration and cooperation. Women have a completely different view of what "team"
means—how teams should function and what their objective is.

Women almost always try to advance projects by achieving consensus. Does this sound like an unfounded generalization based on traditional ideas about women? Lots of people might think so. But it's true. And not only is it true, it constitutes one of women's greatest strengths in business. In fact, women's "natural" model looks a lot like the new paradigm that many of today's businesses are trying to adopt.

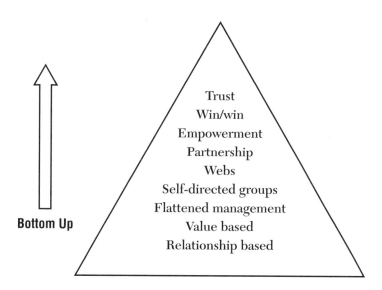

The New Business Model

The Traditional Model for business is a fish tank in which women don't thrive. The difficulty most men have in recognizing and appreciating this is that they seldom, if ever, find themselves in a similar situation in the workplace.

Nathan, a young male manager, and the only man on the board of The Body Shop, an international skin products company, told me he was unfamiliar with his company's way of making decisions. The company operated on the new paradigm, a collaborative model. Whereas the Traditional Model focuses on a goal and on finding the means to achieve the goal, the New Model focuses on empowerment, building trust, and collaboration. This model was completely counterintuitive to Nathan. "I can't believe we ever get anything done," he said. But they do.

For women, the traditional working environment feels like a kind of silent, ongoing culture shock. That's probably why almost half the women I meet in workshops are considering leaving their jobs. "The workplace just isn't conducive to valuing women," they constantly tell me.

Women's culture shock usually starts after college or graduate school, the last time men and women work together in a genuine team spirit before heading out into the "real" world. In the workplace, men naturally shift to the hierarchical mode. They feel comfortable in that sport/games model. Men's teams have "leaders," "stars," and a distinct structure from the outset. The teams exist only to meet targets, to "win." Terms like "partnership" and "team-building" have become very stylish in the business world these days, but in reality, men's idea of "teamwork" still follows the same old model—namely, that a good team player is someone who follows the boss. Today, for many women, and for an increasing number of men, this corporate model no longer works.

Everyone's Problem

That's where today's workplace is. Everywhere, large numbers of people are unhappy at work. A recent international study by Gallup offers a good illustration of how low worker morale really is. The study questioned 1.7 million workers in 101 companies in 63 different countries. The workers were asked whether they "felt they had the opportunity to do their best every day" at their job. Only *20 percent* of employees said yes! Only one-fifth of today's workers feel they are getting the opportunity to put their personal strengths and talents to work. The study found that the longer the employees stayed in their jobs and the higher they climbed the traditional career ladder, the less they felt they were giving their "best stuff" at work. When 80 percent of employees feel they aren't making the contribution they could be making at their jobs, there's clearly a problem.

You're probably thinking, "Okay, maybe there is a problem. But it's only in traditional businesses or old-fashioned companies." That's a modern myth. Everywhere I see men and women working together, they are encountering the same problems. Even modern high-tech companies aren't exempt from the rule.

The common wisdom is that working women want to spend more time with their families. But the reality is that everyone does, men and women alike. What many of the women I meet really want from their work—and what they're not getting—is the feeling that they are doing something meaningful and that they are valued. A lot of men I meet feel this way too.

The problem in today's workplace is not a "women's problem." Companies, organizations, and associations of all types need to learn how to make use of both men's and women's strengths. That's the only way to change the water we swim in so that everyone will be happy and productive.

Leaders in very few of the companies I meet understand that the issue in today's workplace is not just about "treating women better" but about changing the environment of their company so women, and men, will thrive and flourish.

Mike, senior manager at a large accounting firm, is one of many men who have told me how concerned they are about getting and keeping professional women. "I know there's something about the environment that alienates women," he told me. "It's not discrimination, really. It's just subtle differences in the way women are treated."

Mike is among the more enlightened business leaders with respect to gender awareness. These precious few already understand that gender communication problems are a business problem. They know the growth in their company—their aquarium—will be held back unless they find a way to change the water.

The Solution? Fresh Water

So where do we start? The first step in overcoming gender-based misunderstanding is to realize that men and women really are different. That's a surprisingly tough concept to get across these days. Over time, the prevailing wisdom has held that "equal" means "the same." It doesn't. Men and women don't think the same way. They don't communicate the same way. They don't hear the same things when they are spoken to and they don't mean the same things when they speak. A lot of the time, we just think we understand when we don't. Miscommunication feeds misinterpretation.

It's always tempting for women to say, "Men have to change. That will solve all our problems." But that way of thinking won't get either women or men ahead. It's a mistake to think that if women are losing out, men are winning. It's not a zero-sum game. Gender-based miscommunication hurts everyone. The current environment is not men's fault, and the way to fix it is not as simple as "getting men to change." As much as men need to understand how women think and communicate, women need to understand the same about men.

Both genders need to understand where the other is coming from, and they need to be able to walk a mile in each other's shoes. The only way to do that is by understanding how we are different. We think differently. We assimilate information differently. And we communicate differently.

This book is about changing the water in the aquarium. It's about turning a no-win situation into a win-win situation. The idea is not to throw out the old model once and for all and replace it with the new model. There are situations in business where the old model still works well—where hierarchical, centralized decision-making is very effective. But the *environment* has to change. How do we change it? By developing congruence between the old and the new, recognizing the special strengths men and women both bring to the table, and knowing how and when to put those strengths to use. When you do that, the environment will change. Not only will women be happier, everyone will. You'll create a work environment that

- ✓ Encourages open and honest communication
- ✓ Fosters the continual development of all employees
- ✓ Recognizes and appreciates everyone's strengths
- ✓ Maximizes everyone's engagement and productivity
- ✓ Applies an inclusive, not exclusive, approach to gender difference
- ✓ Respects the individual and values integrity

The secret to changing the environment is understanding gender difference. As you'll see in the following chapters, a lot of gender communication problems boil down to some simple differences between us. At least, those simple differences plant the seed from which the problems grow. I've observed the differences over and over again in my work. They are things you have all told me about yourselves.

Until we understand our differences, we will keep misinterpreting each other. But that change starts with you. Until you understand how life looks and sounds through the eyes and ears of the other gender, you will continue to misunderstand it.

The good news? At the end of your trip through these pages—through gender difference and back again—you'll see that although men and women are different, there's a lot more uniting us than dividing us. People basically want the same thing from their work: the feeling that they are contributing and that they have the opportunity as individuals to learn and grow.

In the next chapter, you'll take the first step on the gender journey, and that means taking a good, hard look at how much you actually know about gender difference.

2

How Gender Intelligent Are You?

Our resistance to generalizing or stereotyping propels us into a well-intentioned form of denial.

—Carol Gilligan, Ph.D., *In a Different Voice*

How can you change the environment in which you work? It sounds like a monumental task, but it starts with a pretty simple process: figuring out *your* role in the problem. To do that, you first must take an honest look at your own level of gender intelligence—in other words, you have to face how much you actually know about how different the other gender is versus how much you *think* you know.

Like many people who attend my workshops, you may be thinking, "This is a new millennium. We've made progress. Everyone agrees the genders are equal. So what's the problem?" Or you may think, "My mother and father lacked awareness about the differences between men and women, but I don't."

These workshops, typically offered after a client company has assigned us to run a diagnostic on staff awareness of the differences between men and women, are aimed at raising that awareness among both men and women. Most people who attend show up thinking there's no such thing as a gender issue anymore—and therefore no real problem to solve. It's only when workshop attendees take a closer look at their own perceptions that they start to change their minds. Generally speaking, men and women fall along a continuum of what I call the four Stages of Awareness. They are

1. Enlightened Denial
2. Recognition/Awareness
3. Confusion/Frustration
4. Partnership/Congruence

Men's Stages of Awareness

The first quiz is for men. Consider this an opportunity to take a hard look at your own degree of awareness, without anyone criticizing or blaming you for how you think. The more honest you are about your feelings, the more you'll get out of it. Fortunately, this is not a final exam that will determine your grade in anything at all; there's no passing or failing in gender difference. It's all about learning.

Questionnaire for Men

	Never	Sometimes	Often
Time will take care of things.	☐	☐	☐
We've already employed more women.	☐	☐	☐
You have to be so politically correct these days.	☐	☐	☐
I treat everybody the same.	☐	☐	☐
We have the policies in place.	☐	☐	☐
We have quotas in place.	☐	☐	☐
I don't discriminate!	☐	☐	☐
It's the system; I can't change the system.	☐	☐	☐
Women just don't thrive in this environment.	☐	☐	☐
Women leave to have children.	☐	☐	☐
Women primarily leave due to "work-life issues."	☐	☐	☐
We already have plenty of women managers.	☐	☐	☐
It's not about gender; it's about personality styles.	☐	☐	☐
It's not about gender; it's about diversity.	☐	☐	☐
It's a male-dominated environment.	☐	☐	☐
There is too much focus on women.	☐	☐	☐
It's our company's culture.	☐	☐	☐
Equal opportunity will ensure fairness.	☐	☐	☐
It's the older generation who doesn't get it.	☐	☐	☐
This is not a place I want my daughter to work.	☐	☐	☐
The work is tough; you have to be available 24/7.	☐	☐	☐
It's time to move beyond gender.	☐	☐	☐

If you answered "sometimes" or "often" to most of these statements, you are in Stage One or Stage Two of gender awareness. Stay the course; that will change. The whole idea of this book is to bring you to the highest level, Stage Four. And when you get there, you'll not only be able to change your entire work environment, but you'll also love the change!

If none of these four Stages of Awareness is a perfect fit for you, don't worry. When you've read the descriptions of all of them, you'll understand where you fit. And nothing is written in stone. You may be in Stage One today and Stage Four tomorrow, and then find yourself back in Stage Two the next day, depending on the circumstances. That's normal. The name of the game is to move toward Stage Four more and more often, and in more trying and pressured circumstances, until you arrive there to stay as naturally as breathing—that is, until Stage Four is your new normal.

Your job now is to examine the assumptions about women you carry around with you. You may not be conscious of it, but you have plenty of such assumptions. And women have them about you. Once you've taken your assumptions out of the closet and faced them, you will be ready to move on to the next three chapters, where you will see how the other gender thinks, and you will learn to really listen to what women are saying. Then you'll be ready for the tools to improve your relations with the opposite gender in your work environment.

Stage One—Denial

In the context of gender intelligence, there are two forms of denial. The first, Denying the Denial, is the classic stonewall: "There's no problem here. I yell at everyone the same." But there is also another, more sophisticated, form of denial that can be more difficult to identify. I call it Enlightened Denial. It happens when you think you know all there is to know about gender issues. Men in this form of denial have often made some superficial changes to their language or behavior and think this is enough to do the trick.

Denying the Denial

Men in this first type of denial usually work in the male business environment, and they are honestly convinced that women's experiences are the same as men's. These men don't think women's concerns warrant any special attention. They think more or less like this:

- ✓ "We're all here to do a job, and women should be treated exactly the same as men."
- ✓ "Women say they're equal. I had to pay my dues. So should they!"
- ✓ "Why should a woman get any special treatment?"
- ✓ "Women shouldn't get something for nothing, and I won't give up what I've earned."

Rob, an executive in a technology company, made a typical denial remark. "There's no gender issue at work. It's just different personalities. And you can't change people's personalities. If one of our brokers is having a bad day and gets a little out of line, why should that be such a big deal?" Other comments typical of men in denial are "We've got women. Our numbers are good," and "We've got policies for equal opportunity, work-life flexibility, and harassment. There are no problems here." I heard a perfect example of this form of denial from a deputy minister who was arguing with a colleague about the principle of pay equity. "Women get paid less than men because they *choose* to work in low-paying jobs!" he said. It was classic Stage One reasoning. "They are the secondary income earner; we must be the breadwinners…."

Men in denial are comfortable with the current working environment. They usually don't think there is such a thing as "women's issues" in the workplace. "We're all the same. We're all professionals," they say. These men are often successful and in positions of power, or they are heading in that direction. They don't see any reason for change.

Enlightened Denial

Men in Enlightened Denial often believe they understand the gender "issue." Their assumptions run something like this:

- ✓ "I know all about this gender stuff. I'm an enlightened man. I don't discriminate."
- ✓ "The problem is the old guys."

Men in Enlightened Denial often see successful women around them and conclude that the world has changed. "The problem has been solved," they say. As one U.S. colonel put it, "We have two female colonels. They made it, so this problem is in the past!" Although these men may have dealt with gender issues in their past, their attitude has resulted in a form of denial that closes doors to further discussion and presents a formidable obstacle to gaining understanding or increasing awareness of gender difference. Men in Enlightened Denial also believe gender problems can be solved simply by making small changes in language or behavior. These men often have the best of intentions, but they tend to be stuck in a rudimentary understanding of a few of the high-profile gender issues they hear about in the news.

Stage Two—Recognition/Awareness

Men in this stage realize that there is a fundamental difference in the way the world operates for and is experienced by men and women. They want to fix the difference, but they don't know how. Men in this stage don't yet think it's necessary to change the status quo; they see their "male model" work environment, which they enjoy, as the obvious standard. You hear these men say:

- ✓ "Really, I had no idea women felt that way."
- ✓ "I see the problem, but what can I do? It's the system. I can't change the system."
- ✓ "OK, just give me three things that I can do and I'll do them."
- ✓ "Well I do get it, but it's the old boys who don't."

Men often get into Stage Two when their assumptions have been challenged by an event in their personal lives. These men have often witnessed the experiences of a wife who starts or returns to a career, or of a daughter who enters the workforce, and they suddenly start seeing how the working world looks through a woman's eyes. They may see parallels between things their wife or daughter experiences and their own behavior toward female colleagues. Hearing about public cases of discrimination against women can also push men into Stage Two.

What happens when men hear such cases? They can react in one of two ways. Some men in Stage Two quickly revert back to Stage One because they feel forced to live in a politically correct environment to avoid being sued; other men begin to confront their own conscious and unconscious assumptions about women.

Men in this stage have seen a problem and they want to fix it. But these men do not see that the status quo has to change. They still think things can continue in more or less the same way as in the past. Men in Stage Two usually don't stay there for long. Before they know it, they are struggling with Stage Three. "OK, I get it, you keep saying that you feel like an outsider, but what can I do about it?" said a sincere police officer. This is a natural progression to the next stage.

Stage Three—Confusion/Frustration

Men in this stage recognize that the world works differently for women and men, but they feel as if they are being blamed for the misdeeds of all men throughout history. In Stage Two, they thought they had gender issues all cleared up, but now they feel like they've tried everything and nothing has worked. They feel they are trapped in a no-win situation where they make endless concessions but get the same negative reactions from women. This can be a very frustrating stage for men. They tend to sound plaintive:

✓ "We've made every effort, we have the policy, and we have a women's network in place."

✓ "I don't know what else we can do; maybe it's just the nature of the work."

✓ "We've already addressed this a long time ago; it's time to move on."

Many men in companies that have had a hard time holding on to talented women turn to quick-fix solutions—a policy to hire more women, for example. When these strategies flounder after a short period, men become frustrated and confused.

When that happens, men often slip back into a form of denial fueled by the frustration. "Maybe women just can't cope with it," these men suggest. "We've tried to employ more women. We've had an Equal Opportunities policy in place for years. But the women either leave or just don't advance."

As one senior manager at a major investment bank told me, "There's nothing we can do. Women stay in personal and corporate banking, but not in investment banking. We're never going to change that!"

Vijay, a mid-level manager at a consulting firm, was a typical Stage Three man. "Women can't make it in this company," he declared. "Three years ago we had five women; now there's only one left. When the going gets tough, they just leave." It's not just individual men who experience this stage. I deal with entire companies who are in Stage Three.

Jason, the chief executive officer of a famous investment firm, is a classic example of someone in Stage Three. "We are losing ground with women," he said. "A few years ago our numbers looked fine, but we've slipped. We seem to either lose them altogether or they move to another side of the bank." Bitter after all his work to employ and promote women had failed, Jason was extremely frustrated, and he found himself having a new kind of conversation with his colleagues. Instead of moving to Stage Four by recognizing the need for changing the work environment, he reverted back to Stage One. "Maybe it's just the nature of the beast! Maybe women just can't thrive in the investment side of our bank," he said.

Stage Three can be so frustrating that men simply find it easier to revert back into the "comfort zone" of Stage One. But some continue taking a stand and move on to Stage Four.

Stage Four—Partnership/Congruence

Men in Stage Four have recognized that women's experience in the workplace differs drastically from their own. They have stopped seeing women's issues as a zero-sum game, and they have stopped trying to "fix" gender issues just by changing their language and their behavior. Men in Stage Four don't look at "women's issues" as "something we have to put up with." They have stopped seeing women as a class and see women's issues as people issues. They understand that everyone can win when gender differences are recognized and understood. Their thinking has evolved to the point where they can affirm, as one told me, that "if we understand women better, everyone will benefit. I can personally continue my efforts in the workplace in a more inclusive and empowering way."

Matthew is a manager at IBM who had worked hard on achieving real gender awareness by actively changing the workplace environment within his department. "This is not just the flavor of the month," he said. "We are going to make lasting positive changes around here!" He listened to both men and women and collaborated on efforts to create win-win solutions. He could see how these efforts had improved the working atmosphere and communication among his employees. It had even affected the many cultural differences that also existed. These benefits were reflected in a survey carried out by the corporate Human Resources department. "Everyone is doing a better job. The men are also seeing it as a positive change for them," Matthew said.

Getting to Stage Four isn't always easy, as Manu, a director of a pharmaceutical company, told me. "I had to struggle with the whole thing for a while without giving up," he said, "but I can clearly see the positive strides we have all made; we clearly enjoy working together more. Even the most difficult of tasks has become easier." Manu saw clearly what needed to be done and implemented mutually beneficial policies. The key to Stage Four is ongoing commitment. Men in this stage are ready to listen and keep listening. They have understood that the only way to learn is to get feedback from other people, from their closest women friends, their spouses, or their colleagues. They have accepted that change is necessary. They are truly listening to what women have to say.

One particularly honest man in the onset of this stage admitted, "I don't have a clue as to what it's like to be a woman!" He approached gender difference inquisitively, like a child, taking nothing for granted.

It can be frustrating if you are trying to "solve" something, but not if you are just trying to "learn."

Men, you might not go through Stage Three. Many men go straight from Stage Two to Stage Four. But Stage Two, the awareness stage, is particularly challenging. If you are in this stage, you may find yourself using new information about gender difference simply to update old stereotypes. You end up with a sophisticated form of stereotyping. For instance, you've learned that "women personalize things," and you go on to make this new stereotype an excuse for inaction, not a tool for further understanding.

But men in Stage Four don't fall into that trap. They have achieved real partnerships with women. They are beyond just working on changing their language and behavior. If you're a Stage Four man, you understand that women and men are equal, but not the same. You are aware that women have unique strengths and you know that when men and women share perspectives, it can be mutually empowering. You are comfortable with women's authentic style, and you are comfortable with your own authentic style.

You may think that Stage Four is an impossible ideal, but read on. In the next two chapters, you will probably find yourself spending time in all the Stages of Awareness, interchangeably. When you get to the end of this book, though, you'll be ready to live in Stage Four—and enjoy the benefits.

Women's Stages of Awareness

Women often think that it's men who don't know anything and it's men who need to change. But nothing could be further from the truth! Women can be in Denial too, and women's Denial does the same damage as men's, provoking misunderstandings that feed misconceptions and leave everyone frustrated. Before you read about Women's Stages of Awareness, try this Gender Awareness Quiz to test your own assumptions and prejudices.

Questionnaire for Women

	Never	Sometimes	Often
Time will take care of things.	☐	☐	☐
It's an "old boys club."	☐	☐	☐
Men don't care.	☐	☐	☐
Men just don't understand.	☐	☐	☐
You have to challenge and confront men.	☐	☐	☐
Women have to be more tough and demanding.	☐	☐	☐
Senior management doesn't see it as a priority.	☐	☐	☐
Men wish for "the good old days."	☐	☐	☐
It's the system; I can't change the system.	☐	☐	☐
It's a male-dominated environment.	☐	☐	☐
It's not related to gender; it's personality styles.	☐	☐	☐
It's the corporate culture here.	☐	☐	☐
I'm not a feminist.	☐	☐	☐
It's more about diversity.	☐	☐	☐
Isn't it time to move beyond gender?	☐	☐	☐

If you've answered "sometimes" or "often" to most of these statements, you are in the lower levels of awareness. And now you'll see why.

Stage One—Denial/Unawareness

Typically, women in this stage don't even want to hear about gender difference. They equate the notion of being different from men with the notion of being weaker than men. Many women in Stage One have spent their lives trying to prove they are as good as, or better than, men in the workplace. They have shown they can make it on the same terms as men. To do this, they had to disprove stereotypes about women. They had to fight traditional attitudes among their coworkers. They attended leadership workshops where they were taught strategies like "don't say excuse me," and "boom your voice," and "keep in control, make sure no one interrupts you, be the first to interrupt." In other words, they learned to act like men.

Women in denial say:

✓ "I don't see any specific challenges with gender."
✓ "I agree that we may have challenges, but they have to do with personalities and styles, and you can't change that!"
✓ "Time is taking care of things."

These women think the male model is "just the way things are." They don't imagine that things can work differently, that there can be a different model. Many women in denial are locked into a paradigm where being different is equated with being less—less capable, less talented, less appreciated, less successful. Women's differences have long been used as a justification for keeping them suppressed. Successful women are afraid that if they talk about difference, it will be used against them. "I just want to leave that stuff behind and do my job," they say. I've seen successful women go to great lengths to wipe out differences that might "mark" them as women. One female politician actually had her assistant carry her handbag for her when she came to high-profile presentations! "This is so I can march in just like men do!" she said.

Ashley, a powerful sales executive, told me, "I'm not interested in putting this gender label on things. That's an excuse some women use. You just have to be like one of the boys!" Ashley seemed to see herself as a man in women's clothes; she had taken all the assertiveness and get-tough leadership training to fit in. But both men and women feared her. Women in this form of Stage One tend to feel that they scratched and clawed their way up, that everyone has to go through it, and that women can't expect special treatment. "They have to meet our criteria," one told me.

Among some younger women, there's a different type of Stage One. In college or university, men and women are taught the same skills in exactly the same way. So it's hard to discern the differences. Young women are convinced that young men are more or less like them, and that they will not act differently once they join the workplace. They haven't seen the patterns yet. When they experience patronizing behavior from older male colleagues, they tell themselves it's just an exception to the rule, a relic from an older generation.

Women in this stage often call their work "the treadmill"; they believe in "sticking it out." You just get up, go to work, and don't make too many waves.

Stage Two—Recognition/Awareness

Women in Stage Two, like men in Stage Two, recognize that there is a fundamental difference in how women and men perceive things, but they don't yet want to change the status quo. They are prepared to continue working in the traditional hierarchical male structure without questioning or challenging it.

Surprisingly, although most women talk about the problems they have when working with men, they tend to believe deep down that their problems are somehow their own fault—that is, until they get to Stage Two. In Stage Two, women see and feel the challenges caused by gender difference. They discover that there is a larger cultural problem, and that many of their problems are not their own fault. Justine, a researcher at a pharmaceuticals company, told me, "I used to think the problems I had at work were just my own fault. But after reading some research, I talked to other women, and now I see I'm really not alone."

Women in this stage say:

- ✓ "I thought I just had to work harder and prove myself more, but now I see that lots of other women feel the same way I do."
- ✓ "Well, maybe there are gender differences, but I see them more at home than at work."
- ✓ "I just don't want to be labeled as the feminist or the complainer."

Women in Stage Two have a sense of what's wrong, but they don't yet have the resolve to change things. They're not interested in challenging the way things are done. These women don't want to differentiate themselves too much from men. They are confident they can "work around" the corporate structure. They are sure they will be able to find solutions on their own. "I can cope with it," they often say. They see feminist positions as "extreme," so they don't join women's organizations in their company. "Feminism doesn't really represent me or my voice," they say.

Many women under 35 are in Stage Two. These women recognize the problems caused by gender difference, but like women in Stage One, they think time will resolve them. "When the older men leave, things will improve," they say. Many female service industry workers are also in Stage Two. They recognize there are differences in how men and women work, but their solution is to create a comfortable niche where they function well.

Stage Three—Confusion/Frustration

Women in Stage Three either feel forced to be resigned to their situation or they begin to plan an exit strategy. They may have made several attempts to deal with specific situations, but without tangible results. These are their mantras:

- ✓ "I know what's wrong, but everyone seems to tell me just to accept the way things are!"
- ✓ "It's the system; you can only do so much."
- ✓ "I've tried on my own to improve things, but that's the way things are."

Many women in Stage Three have attained high positions within the existing corporate structure. They have experienced a great deal of stress trying to deal with gender issues in their workplace, and now they have just "had it." They are either ready to leave their jobs and do something else, or they "quit and stay," just working their basic hours each day, without any enthusiasm, passion, or commitment.

Women in Stage Three don't want to fight the system. Or they feel profound ambivalence about what to do, what their role should be, and whether or not they should be leading a revolution for change. They feel disempowered. Karen, a career police officer who belongs to two minorities—women and African-Americans—told me that new employees would eventually have to "wake up and smell the coffee." She said, "That's just the way things are around here. The system is what it is, and I'm not going to be able to change it. I've been at this for 15 years, and nothing has changed."

Many women in Stage Three consider making a career shift by starting their own business; some look to work at a smaller company, convinced the grass is greener in a more compact environment. One woman in Stage Three, who worked for a brewery, told me she was tired of the "testosterone bouncing off the walls" at her office. It seemed impossible to change the culture. She was tired of trying to find her place in an environment that was male-centered. Like many women in Stage Three, she yearned for a job where she could be herself, for an environment where she felt valued. She wanted to do something she felt made a difference.

Like Sandra, the ace litigator for our law firm in Chapter 1, women who are firmly embedded in Stage Three usually choose to vote with their feet.

Stage Four—Partnership/Congruence

At the onset of Stage Four, women have overcome the ambivalence they felt in Stage Three. They have seen that there is really no option. It's either the status quo or action, and they have decided to take action. Women in Stage Four have let go of the past and are focused on the future. They are starting with a clean slate. They have become intentional and not reactive about gender difference. They feel a sense of responsibility for their situation instead of a sense of resignation. They are willing to take a stand and work toward creating an inclusive environment at work. Their watchwords have changed:

✓ "The status quo doesn't have to last forever."
✓ "Now both men and women are making the effort, and we can all see the progress."
✓ "Instead of tolerating the differences, we are actually using our differences to our advantage."
✓ "I actually look forward to going to work now."

Women in Stage Four are open to possible ways of improving their situation, and they are interested in making the best of things. They experience a sense of empowerment and often join committees or initiate task forces on gender issues.

The risk in Stage Four? It can easily lead women back to Stage Three. Women's networks can often re-create the same kind of gender exclusion that women set out to change in the first place! Being pro-active can lure women into an us-versus-them mentality. I encourage women who have decided to take action to include men on their committees or task force. "What's wrong with just being a group of women?" some might say in reaction. That reaction is a sign that they are in, or slipping back to, Stage Three. When women welcome my advice on inclusion, it means they are truly in Stage Four.

Later on in this stage, women reap the benefits of their efforts to be inclusive. They have a sense of commonality, but they now understand the differences between women and men. Gender difference doesn't look like a "problem to solve" anymore. They see the advantages in men's and women's differences. They see both men's and women's potential strengths. They understand the potential of real partnership between men and women. They've grasped the truth that there is power in the differences between genders.

Women in Stage Four have left behind blame. They don't have to complain, "You don't understand!" to the men around them; rather, they feel confident enough to suggest, "Let's try to walk in each other's shoes for a while." They understand that men and women often have different perceptions and strengths that can complement one another if the genders work together. Like men in Stage Four, women in Stage Four have progressed to the point of seeing gender differences as a win-win situation.

"It's a much nicer, richer way to get the job done!" said Anna, a bank executive in Stage Four, who had decided to take action. "We are now really open to listening, communicating, and resolving things as they come up! What a difference from when we used to take sides and argue and debate about who was wrong and who was right! Better still, our results speak louder than words!"

At what stage do most women tend to stay? You probably guessed it—Stage Three. In that stage, you have recognized that there is a problem but feel powerless to do anything about it. You are fixated on the problem, and you will check the surveys and do the research to find evidence of how big the problem is. Or you try to "do your bit" and end up frustrated and bitter. At this point, most women either revert to Stage Two or vote with their feet and leave. In other words, they are stuck in the problem identification stage.

How do you get past the problem identification stage? That will unfold in the pages that follow. In the next chapter, I'll show you how men and women are different. Then I'll take you behind the scenes and let you listen to men and women talking honestly about what it feels like to work together. If you listen carefully, with an open mind—and if you put aside your assumptions—you'll see how differences create misunderstandings. You'll see how the spiral of misunderstanding gets started.

Then, once you understand how gender difference creates misunderstandings and have learned to walk in each others' shoes, you'll be ready to pick up the tools that can overcome those misunderstandings and make you at home in Stage Four.

3

The Science of Gender Difference

Facts are stubborn things....

—John Adams, second president of the U.S.

Until the year 1990, women were routinely excluded from medical research—at least in the United States—even when the subject was something as female-centric as the effect of estrogen on heart disease. In that year, however, prodded by feminist activism, the U.S. government's National Institutes of Health opened the Office of Research on Women's Health and ignited a revolution in our understanding of gender-related differences in human physiology and health. Advances followed—in diseases unique to women or with a higher prevalence in women than in men as well as in diseases in which women present differently from men.

Equally illuminating were the researches into the differences in the ways men's and women's brains work. Scientists observed that men's brains are, on average, up to 10 percent larger than women's. They also noted that certain parts of women's brains contain more connections between neurons, the cells that transmit and receive messages to and from the brain. In women, for instance, the part of the brain associated with language skills contains up to 11 percent more brain cells than the corresponding part in men's brains.

The research revolution that had begun as a demand for equality—women insisting on their share of government research dollars—had become a fascinating look at why equality doesn't mean uniformity. In medicine, neuroscience, biology, cultural anthropology, and psychology, study findings repeatedly showed differences in how the two genders acquire and process information. For example, women's brains are particularly adept at verbal fluency, remembering lists of words or paragraphs, or recalling landmarks on a route. For spatial tasks, like mentally rotating images, orienting oneself in a closed space, and navigating through a route, men's brains excel.

Certainly, anyone who has ever watched kids on a playground— or shepherded their children through adolescence—knows well that boys and girls think and behave in gender-specific ways. Some of these differences derive from upbringing, but many may also be the result of evolution. As anthropologist Helen Fisher shows in *The First Sex: The Natural Talents of Women and How They Are Changing the World*,[1] whereas men's brains evolved to make them able hunters, women's evolved to make them able gatherers. While men spent their time fighting to be "at the top," women spent theirs "taking care." Men's brains adapted to focus on a goal, while women's brains adapted to take in a lot of stimuli as they searched for food, built relationships, and monitored their children—all at once.

And now the latest technological advances in the field of neuroscience have made it possible for scientists virtually to watch men and women's brains at work. What have they discovered from this inside look? Confirmation that the brains of men and women are different and that those differences influence almost everything we do.

Tendencies, Not Absolutes

This chapter explores some of those differences in brain structure and chemistry and the influences they exert on the why and how of men and women acting the way they do—specifically, acting the way they do on the job, whatever the nature of the job, and whether they work on a factory floor or in a corporate office. But it's important to understand from the outset that when we speak of behavioral differences, we're describing a bell curve of gender-related *tendencies*. This means that there is a distribution of behavior along a continuum, and that a greater number of people in the distribution exhibit tendencies that fall toward the middle, or norm. For example, if we organized everyone on a continuum from intuitive to factual, more women

---

1. Dr. Helen Fisher, *The First Sex: The Natural Talents of Women and How They Are Changing the World* (New York: The Ballantine Publishing Group, 2000).

would fall toward the intuitive side of the midpoint and more men toward the factual.

If you place these two bell curves alongside each other, you'll notice a sizeable difference between the *average* tendency of men and the *average* tendency of women.

Intuitive   Factual

Given the distribution of human dynamics along this curve, it would be both inaccurate and an overgeneralization to claim that all women act one way and all men act another. After all, there is some overlap on the graph. In fact, research suggests that about 20 percent of men and women—one in five—are hardwired more like the opposite gender. But what is revealed within the *predominant* tendencies—the predispositions of men and women—is both striking and meaningful.

Women and Men Have Different Brains

The brain is naturally divided down the middle to form two hemi-spheres. In general, the left hemisphere is dominant in language, pro-cessing what we hear and how we communicate. It's also the source of linear, logical, and serial thinking. When we need to retrieve a fact, the left brain pulls it from our memory.

The right hemisphere is mainly in charge of spatial abilities, face recognition, and processing music. The brain's right side also helps us comprehend visual imagery and make sense of what we see. It plays a role in language—particularly in interpreting context, abstract thought, and a person's tone—and in how we deal with our emotions.

Men tend to be sequential in their use of right and left brain. Women's abilities, due to a gender-specific density of neural connections linking the two hemispheres, source from both simultaneously. Different.

A study under the direction of Associate Professor Ragini Verma, in the Section of Biomedical Image Analysis in the Department of Radiology at the University of Pennsylvania, mapped the difference. To look at how brains are wired in males and females, Verma and her team, representing such disciplines as psychology and neurology as well as imaging and analytics, used a technique called *diffusion tensor imaging* to map neural connections in the brains of 428 males and 521 females aged 8 to 22.[2] "Scans showed greater connectivity between the left and right sides of the brain in women, while the connections in men were mostly confined to individual hemispheres," the Penn study found. "The only region where men had more connections between the left and right sides of the brain was in the cerebellum, which plays a vital role in motor control."

Researchers studying the corpus callosum, the band of fibers connecting the two hemispheres, confirmed the findings of the Penn study. They concluded that the corpus callosum is as much as 25 percent larger on average in women's brains than in men's, is shaped differently, and contains more nerve fibers. This is the gender-specific density of neural connections referred to by Verma's team, and this means that women's brains have a distinctively different capacity to travel back and forth easily between their left and right sides.[3]

In practical terms, the question came down to whether men and women use their brains differently to do the same tasks, an exploration that the Penn study vigorously pursued. Dr. Ruben Gur, professor of psychology and director of the Brain Behavior Laboratory at the University of Pennsylvania and a coauthor of the Verma brain study, reported on tests tracking the 949 men and women as they were asked to perform a variety of mental tasks. Gur observed that the two genders used different parts of their brains when called upon to perform the same particular task. He also noted that compared to

---

2. Madhura Ingalhalikar, et al., "Sex Differences in the Structural Connectome of the Human Brain," *Proceedings of the National Academy of Sciences* (January 2014).

3. Louann Brizendine, *The Female Brain* (New York: Three River Press, Crown Publishing, 2007), 64–65.

men's brains, women's brains were almost never "off"; he noted as much blood-flow activity in a resting woman's brain as in a thinking man's. "On average," Gur found, "a woman's brain has 15 to 20 percent more blood flow, and the rate of neuron firing in women's brains is higher."[4] Again, more connections being made, more neurons launching signals around the body. Different.

Some scientists also believe that the emotional centers are more widely distributed in women's brain than in men's; wider distribution would suggest that in women, emotions link to a lot of other brain processes.

In any event, gender brain differences are there, and it isn't hard to see how they might come into play in our everyday lives—for example, at the office.

What's the Difference?

Imagine that you're heading to a meeting in your boss's conference room. You open the door and walk in. What goes on in your mind as you step through the door?

When I ask this question of men, they invariably tell me that they spot an empty chair and go sit down in it. For men, what's systematic is automatic. They're there for a purpose, and they stick to the ritual.

When I ask women what goes on in their minds when they walk into the room, they talk about the expressions on the faces of the people in the room, their body language, the mood in the room, who's sitting where, who's engaged and who's not. What's automatic to women is to make connections—those restless brains connecting from one hemisphere to the other—and they're as unaware that they're doing it as men are unaware of their fixed focus.

It's as if men look through binoculars and women look through a kaleidoscope. The two genders simply see things differently.

We also listen differently. Simple laboratory tests have shown that men have difficulty filtering out background noises. When there is a lot of noise in the room, or if there are two or more conversations

---

4. Ingalhalikar, et al. "Sex Differences."

going on at the same time, men have trouble hearing what's being said to them. Is this a vestige of life in Neolithic times, when men were the protectors attuned to every vibration in the air? Maybe. What is certain is that women in the same situation get the message clear as a bell. Women can talk on the phone while staying in tune with what is happening around them; for example, they are able to jot down notes on other things to do while still being fully attentive on the phone. This is virtually impossible for men. Dr. Ruben Gur says, "Women often think men aren't listening, that they don't care. In reality, men just have more difficulty hearing what's being said to them."

Maybe because of the differences in the ways we see and hear, men and women also prioritize differently. Women are natural jugglers. A woman once described her office to me as a stove with 12 pots simmering all at once. "They all need stirring at some point or another," she said. The challenge for her was to keep her eye on all of them so she could see which one needed stirring *now*. Women tend to look at work and life this way.

Men don't juggle; they create agendas. That way, they can deal with priorities one at a time, crossing each off the list once it's done. Their aim is to select the most important pot, give it a stir, and then move on to the next one.

A Ride on the Hippocampus

Part of the reason for men and women seeing, hearing, and prioritizing differently is the way their brains assimilate information—specifically, how they absorb information, grasp it, and then process it along. Much of this happens in the hippocampus, the center for memory and emotion, where information goes from short-term memory into long-term memory and influences how we navigate our way around our environment. Studies on brain differences between men and women have shown that the hippocampus is both larger and far more active in women.[5] This tends to explain why women are at ease expressing emotions as well as at recalling intricate details from the past; they have

---

5. Zeenat F. Zaidi, "Gender Differences in the Human Brain: A Review," *The Open Anatomy Journal*, 2 (2010): 37–55.

wider capacity for processing and coding emotional experiences into their long-term memory. That's the source of noticing all those small details and making instantaneous connections to the past—even when they walk into a conference room. It's a kind of multi-thinking.

The less busy hippocampus of men, by contrast, equips them to focus quickly and sharply on the important features of a problem or issue and then remember the facts of the experience rather than its relation to context. That's their way of assimilating information. They zero in on the essence of a situation as automatically as they head for the empty chair in the conference room and claim it for their own.

So the next time you men complain about women bringing a lot of irrelevant hot air into the conversation, think again. Imagine all that connective processing going on in their hippocampus. And women, the next time you rail against men for having blinders on and seeing only one point of view, consider that it's just the way *their* hippocampus works. Complaining and railing serve no purpose; it's just the way the brains of the two genders operate.

Problem Solving, Decision Making, and the Prefrontal Cortex

At the heart of the work we do, whatever it may be, is the need to solve problems, and it is a truism—almost a cliché—that men and women do that very differently. For men, a problem is an adversary—an opposing defender who needs to be blocked, a sales target that has to be achieved in the next quarter, some sort of moving target that needs to be slowed, stopped, and rendered ineffective. So men roll up their sleeves, get down to work, isolate the problem, analyze it, devise a solution, and act. Fast.

Multi-thinking women take a different approach, focusing more on the how than on the what of the goal. With many parts of their brain working at once, they naturally tend to see the problem in many colors. They note patterns and connections that suggest nuances for analysis, and they take time to explore all the angles.

Of course, each gender finds the other gender frustrating when they're trying together to solve the same problem. Women see men as just barreling ahead, oblivious to the subtleties that can affect the outcome. And men see women as just wasting time discussing a topic way too thoroughly.

The differences in brain physiology show up in the decision-making process as well, but here, the main player is the prefrontal cortex. It is the part of our brains that controls judgment and behavior—that directs actions toward goals—and it is not only larger in women than in men but also develops earlier in girls than in boys.[6] It's why young boys are more exploratory, more mischievous, and sometimes more careless than young girls.

By the time the young girls have grown up, the prefrontal cortex, as prize-winning science writer Deborah Blum put it in her book, *Sex on the Brain*, "is also the source of enhanced consequential thinking in women, including the prediction of outcomes and expectations."[7] So for women, decision-making is first and foremost about visiting the entire context. Women tend to focus on the long-term and wide-ranging implications of a decision. Seeing connections, they wonder how a decision will affect the work of other departments or the relationship they have built with a client. They instinctively connect the dots.

Men appreciate the connecting of the dots, but their own focus is on the short-term. The business world is a reactive place. Decisions have to be made and made fast. Again, men naturally tend to isolate the issue so they can get to a decision as quickly as possible.

A former client of mine described these differing decision-making perspectives as a tree house and the ground below. "A woman wants to go up in the tree house and look down on the whole scene to see how it all connects," he said, "while men just want to stay on the ground where they can do something."

"What I now find useful," this client went on to say, "is to use both perspectives. It enhances our ability to make better and more thorough decisions. So now I actively seek out the views from both the tree house and the ground."

---

6. Deborah Blum, *Sex on the Brain: The Biological Differences between Men and Women* (New York: Viking Publishing, 1997), 63.

7. Blum, "*Sex on the Brain.*"

Feelings

It's pretty well universally agreed that men and women feel things differently. Brain research increasingly confirms this. Remember the corpus callosum, the band of fibers connecting the right and left hemispheres of the brain? Because this is thinner in a man's brain than in a woman's, with fewer connecting fibers, some scientists suggest the flow of information from one hemisphere to the other is not as fluid in men. And since the right hemisphere houses the emotions, while the left is home to the power to express emotions in speech, a slow flow between hemispheres is bound to decelerate men's ability to express their emotions. The information just doesn't flow as easily from the emotional right side of the brain to the verbal left side of the brain. But in women, the corpus callosum is thick and dense, and while this means emotions and their expression are easy, it also makes women less able to separate emotion from reason.

Another difference is found in the insula of the brain. In her revealing book, *The Female Brain*, Louann Brizendine says that the insula, twice as large on average in the female brain as in the male brain, helps women translate "physical sensations and thoughts in the subconscious mind into conscious thoughts that are often richly colored by memories and emotions." It is the insula that "tends to heighten women's perception and intuition, making women far more sensitive than men to the feelings and mood of people and events around them."[8]

Men tend to find it difficult to express their feelings verbally. Women express emotions easily, and, says Fisher in *The First Sex*, they have a propensity to personalize feelings because the emotional connectors in the brain are more linked to the verbal.[9] But in fact the difference isn't just in the way men and women express their emotions; they also are wired to recall emotional memories differently. That is, men and women who experience the same emotional event retrieve the event from memory in different ways.

Dr. Larry Cahill, professor of the Neurobiology and Behavior School of Biological Sciences at the University of California at Irvine,

---

8. Brizendine, *The Female Brain.*

9. Fisher, *The First Sex.*

scanned the brains of men and women while they watched emotionally arousing events and found that the two genders engage different hemispheres of the amygdala, nuclei responsible for forming and storing emotional memories, when they recall those events. Cahill's valuable new insights seem to confirm the detail-versus-big-picture difference in perspectives we've already seen. "In men," Cahill found, "typically only the right amygdala is activated; in women, the left amygdala is activated. Previous research suggests that the right brain processes the general gist of events while the left side focuses on the details.

"This split," Cahill concludes, "could account for differences in the way in which men and women recall emotional fights or events."[10]

Reading Feelings

Wherever and whenever human beings deal with one another—and certainly in the workplace—it is helpful to know if an individual is happy, sad, interested, or bored. What science now tells us is that gender affects how we read the feelings of others as well as how we express our own.

For example, tests show that men don't read or decipher facial expressions—especially the facial expression on a woman's face. Tests also show that women's brains simply do not work as hard as men's do when they are identifying facial expressions. In other words, compared to men, women identify people's emotions without even trying.

The University of Pennsylvania's Ruben Gur demonstrated this when he showed study participants portrait photographs of men and women expressing different emotions. Most of the men could identify the correct emotion on the photographs of men's faces but often had trouble reading the women's faces. Women easily read the emotion on both men's and women's faces.[11]

Emotions are often the first thing women notice. They read emotions even before they listen to what people say. For men, "I'm doing fine" means "I'm doing fine," even if the person who says it is frowning. For women, it's the frown they notice.

---

10. Larry Cahill. "His Brain, Her Brain," *Scientific American* (May 2005).

11. Ingalhalikar, et al. "Sex Differences."

In other words, men read feelings by asking about them and accepting the answers. Women read feelings through instinct and intuition. (Of course, what the studies don't tell is whether either gender or both gets a "true" reading of another's emotions.)

We Deal with Stress Differently

Is there stress at the office? The universal answer is yes, yet gender once again affects how we deal with stress, with women and men responding quite differently. At the simplest level, men either fight or withdraw; if the latter, they effectively go into hiding to focus on the problem. Women tend to react to stress by sharing their feelings; they turn to their friends.

An influential study by UCLA psychologists, published in 2000 in *Psychological Review*,[12] found that women are more likely to deal with stress through what the study authors called "tending and befriending"—that is, by nurturing those around them and reaching out to others. "Tending involves activities designed to protect the self and offspring that promote safety and reduce distress; befriending is the creation and maintenance of social networks that may aid in this process," the study authors wrote.

"Women often seek support to talk out the emotional experience, to process what is happening and what might be done," says Dr. Shelley E. Taylor, lead author of the study, while men "seek an escape activity to get relief from stress, to create a relaxing diversion, to get away." It's why women tend to seek out friends, family, or a support group with whom they can share their stories and thus relieve their stress, while men, by contrast, might want to watch the game, releasing their stressful energy in a mentally challenging and distracting way while enjoying the camaraderie of other men.

Why do women tend and befriend instead of fight or flight? The study concluded that the reason, in large part, is oxytocin, a hormone noted for its role in prosocial behaviors. The tending or befriending

---

12. Shelly E. Taylor, Laura Cousino Kline, et al., "Biobehavioral Responses to Stress in Females: Tend-and-Befriend, Not Fight-or-Flight," *Psychological Review* 107, 3 (2000).

reflex increases the release of oxytocin, and this further counters stress and produces a calming effect, which in turn releases even more oxytocin.

Says Dr. Laura Cousino Klein, one of the coauthors of the UCLA study, "this calming response does not occur in men because testosterone, which men produce in high levels when they're under stress, seems to reduce the effects of oxytocin." Instead they fall back on either fighting back or bottling up the stress and escaping—the fight-or-flight response.

Teamwork: Collaborators or Competitors— or Both?

Women are natural collaborators; men naturally compete and want to win. What does this mean for teamwork on the job? Some studies provide the answer.

Researchers at Emory University took a look at the brain action of women as they played a board game, using an MRI scanner to track blood flow. The scan showed that blood activity in the reward centers of women's brains rose when the women collaborated; the more they collaborated, the more the reward centers were activated. These are the same reward centers that respond to such stimuli as food, money, and drugs. This suggests that women's bodies may have been somehow evolutionarily programmed to find cooperation rewarding.[13] Other researchers have confirmed this finding that women's brains register collaborating as a reward, even when collaboration isn't in a particular woman's own self-interest.

Similar studies of blood activity in men's brains show that, by contrast to women, men feel rewarded when they beat the competition and win the game. As team members, they feel rewarded by being the star of the team or the team leader.

Clearly, the two genders are turned on by different "drugs"; their brains find reward in almost opposite stimuli—men in competition, women in collaboration.

---

13. Yerkes Regional Primate Research Center, Emory University, Atlanta, GA.

What does this tell us about teamwork in a work setting? If it seems to suggest that you need both genders on a team to get the best results, that is a conclusion confirmed in a landmark study coauthored by researchers from MIT's Sloan School of Management, Carnegie Mellon University, and Union College.[14] The study set out to document what it called a "collective intelligence" among people who cooperate well. Six hundred and ninety-nine study participants were formed into teams, which were assigned to work together on tasks ranging from visual puzzles to negotiations, brainstorming, games, and complex, rule-based design exercises.

The study affirmed that collective intelligence extends beyond the individual cognitive abilities of any single member of the group. Instead, groups with the right kind of "internal dynamics" performed well on a wide range of assignments; the conclusion was that a group's collective intelligence accounted for about 40 percent of the variation in performance across a wide range of tasks. As Sloan School Professor of Management Patrick McGovern noted, "We found that there is a general effectiveness, a group collective intelligence, which predicts a group's performance in many situations."

That collective intelligence, the researchers believe, stems from how well the group works together. Interestingly and importantly, the study showed that the tendency to do so is directly linked to the number of women in a group. One reason was the finding that groups with higher levels of "social sensitivity" were more collectively intelligent. "Social sensitivity has to do with how well group members perceive each other's emotions," says Union College's Christopher Chabris, a coauthor of the study. "And teams containing more women demonstrated greater social sensitivity and in turn greater collective intelligence compared to teams containing fewer women."

Not Better, Not Worse, Just Different

Both men and women in our workshops invariably feel a deep sense of relief when we present the science of gender difference.

---

14. Massachusetts Institute of Technology. "Collective Intelligence: Number of Women in Group Linked to Effectiveness in Solving Difficult Problems." *Science Daily* (2 October 2010).

I think they're comforted by the fact that gender difference is more or less coded into our DNA. It means no one needs to feel guilty or deficient because of the way he or she thinks or processes emotions. All those years we may have spent blaming the other sex for not thinking or acting as we do, and it turns out they couldn't help it. We really don't think the same. We don't see reality in the same way. Men's and women's brains work differently, and that's that.

In three decades of studying gender in the corporate world, the patterns I've noticed are absolutely consistent with what scientists say about gender difference, from women's more highly connected brains to men's more focused approach to problem solving. Our differences shape different tendencies, and here is a brief guide to some of the differing tendencies that repeatedly show up in the corporate workplace:

Women tend to...	Men tend to...
Justify.	Carry on regardless.
Look for areas of agreement.	Look for gaps.
Bond in conversations.	Bond in games and tasks.
Find validation in relationships.	Find validation in accomplishments.
Be multi-thinkers—switch topics in conversation.	Be linear thinkers, dealing with one topic at a time.
Have multidimensional insights.	Have linear insights.
Be concerned to feel connected.	Be concerned to stay independent.
Explore every detail before concluding.	Get straight to the point.
Share problems when they want to talk about them.	Share problems only when they want them to be fixed.
First see a problem as "their" problem.	First see a problem as someone else's.
Have personal breakthroughs through validation.	Have personal breakthroughs through struggle and debate.

Given these disparate tendencies, it's no accident that men and women approach the same situations or tasks so differently. Nor is it any wonder that not understanding the difference in approach creates all sorts of misunderstandings, especially because, as you're about to see in the next two chapters, men and women assume that the other sex thinks and acts exactly as they do—and they think that if the other sex doesn't think and act the same as they do, they should. So when a member of the other gender doesn't react the way you would, you jump to conclusions about what they mean.

But—are you beginning to get the picture?—what if the different ways of thinking and acting were brought together? What if men and women together could integrate their separate strengths, could march both sets of brain powers along the same track—seeing both the heart of the matter and the connections to possible consequences, placing both that all-encompassing eye for detail and the homing in on the core issue at the service of a single goal? Wouldn't that potentially define a whole greater than the sum of the parts? Wouldn't appreciating and respecting the different talents of men and women potentially lead to better decisions—in life, yes, but certainly in the workplace? That's what this book is about.

But to get there, we first have to go through the way the world still works today, where inescapable gender differences translate into frustration, confusion, squabbling, clashing, and sometimes confrontation. None of it is good for business or the work at hand. Just listen in the next two chapters as men and women talk openly about how they experience working together—and consider how you, too, may be contributing to gender-based misunderstandings. It's the first step to learning how to resolve such misunderstandings and make a better workplace.

4

Attention, Women: How Men See You—and How They Feel About It

You have to look at a thing from two points of view…to really understand it. The approach is to help us all understand the conversation we find ourselves in and gain insights from each other, not label one way right and the other wrong and thereby further drive a wedge between the sexes….

—Niels Bohr, Danish physicist, Nobel Laureate

It's amazing how little men and women know about one another. I mean, *really* know about one another. Each gender *thinks* it understands the other, but in fact, both men and women are actually suspended—hung up on—a lot of misconceived opinions and assumptions about the other gender. Opinions and assumptions are fine in their place, but they're limited in scope, substance, and usefulness. Why? Because they derive from mapping others' behavior onto our own experience.

When we rely on opinions and assumptions to judge the other gender's behavior, we tend to look for confirmation of what we already believe. We also tend to decide instinctively whether other people are "right" or "wrong" instead of really listening to them.

Opinions are good for making more opinions. Assumptions are good for stopping further exploration or thought. Neither is a tool for learning. In this chapter, the time has come to put aside your opinions and challenge your assumptions. What you're about to receive instead are insights—discoveries we make when we become aware of something that we weren't previously conscious of. Discoveries are about alerting your mind to something entirely new, about grappling with something you never really thought about before, about taking a look at the world through an entirely different pair of eyes. Few of us are paid to have insights, so we don't think about them very much. But insights are exactly what we need if we are to understand the other gender. They are the moments when we say, "Ah-hah!"

At the beginning of the gender intelligence workshops we hold, the men and women are sent into separate rooms so both can talk freely about what's really on their minds without worrying about how to articulate it. This chapter is about what goes on in the men's room—what they say, and the conclusions they come up with. You male readers will relate to many of the comments you are about to read. And women, you will get a chance to stand in the men's shoes. This is your first chance to get some "Ah-hahs" about men. But you'll only be able to do that if you let go of your preconceptions and really listen.

Many women think they understand men through and through. When they hear what men describe in the men's room as their challenges, they are tempted to trivialize them; they find it easy to label men and dismiss them as dinosaurs. Try to resist that easy temptation. I can assure you that the reality is very different from your perception—your misperception.

In fact, in the more than 8,000 gender intelligence workshops we've conducted all over the world, men have always raised the same themes—wherever on earth the workshop was held and whatever the hierarchical level of the participants. Slight cultural differences may at times show up, but these are nuanced variations on the same challenges voiced over and over again. Men truly feel the way they say they do. Yet when women hear men articulate what they see as their challenges, their most common reaction is: "I never realized men felt that way."

Now you can. For women readers, what you'll read in this chapter will enable you to imagine how you would act if you went to work every day with men's concerns. This is your chance to see how the world looks from men's perspective, insight into how they really think. It's an offer you really can't refuse.

In the end, as the great Niels Bohr said at the top of this chapter, it's all about seeing the other's point of view. Only when we stand in each other's shoes and give up the blame game can we gain understanding of one another, and the learning effort must be equal for both men and women.

Men's Top Five Challenges Working with Women

It's difficult to get men to talk about what it feels like to work with women. When I ask the men about their challenges, many close up. "There are no problems," they say. One of my male associate facilitators explains men's reaction this way:

> Men are very, very careful when they talk about women. Sometimes it takes a good five minutes of silence before anyone speaks up. They're concerned about being accused of not being politically correct. When they do start to talk, they say things like, "Don't write this down…. You can't put it that way!" They're very concerned about having this conversation. It's uncomfortable for them.

For women, this alone should provide you with a huge insight into the male perspective on the gender issue. Most women are convinced men aren't interested in talking about it, that they resist the conversation. In fact, men are rather intimidated by the question. Not many women would imagine that the all-powerful male in business would feel he needed to be so cautious when talking about women. But he is, and we'll soon see why.

Here are some of the typical things men say inside the "men's room." If you are a man, feel free to tick off each challenge you can relate to.

✓ Men believe they have to be careful on the subject of women in business or "the gender issue."

✓ Men are confused about "the rules."

✓ Men fear harassment allegations.

✓ Men are concerned about what they perceive as "reverse discrimination," or an overt focus on women.

✓ Men feel blamed.

Challenge 1—Men Believe They Have to Be Careful

Men say:

✓ "I feel as if I'm walking on eggshells around women."

✓ "If I don't know a particular woman, I have to be even more attentive, more cautious. I just don't know how she's going to react!"

✓ "I want to be respectful, but sometimes it blows up in my face."

Many men report feeling always a little bit on guard around women. They don't know how women will react in situations in which their reactions are predictable. As one lawyer told me, "If my colleague Matt does a bad job in court one day, I can just tell him, 'Matt, you did a lousy job in there today,' and we move on. With a female colleague I just never know. I mean I feel that I have to ease into the criticism slowly to get her to get the point. Why? Because I know she'll take it personally. Matt will just shrug it off."

Time and again, men report that

✓ Women remember everything, and "things come back to haunt you years after they happened."

✓ Women take things personally and overreact to things that men would just put behind them and move on from.

✓ They worry about how to deliver criticism to female colleagues without offending them.

✓ They just don't know where women are coming from.

✓ They fear women will think they are being condescending or discriminating if they try to help them or "act protective."

✓ They don't know whether to compliment a woman on her appearance or not. On the one hand, it seems like a courteous thing to do. But then she might take it the wrong way.

✓ They are afraid of women crying!

Women's Reaction

Women are always surprised to learn that men spend so much time thinking about these things. And they are amazed at how afraid men are of making women cry. As one woman put it, "I had no idea how concerned men were about how to act with women, how to make good impressions on women, how to avoid offending women. I just assumed men never thought about it."

Of course, it's not all roses. Women are a little surprised when they hear men talk about being careful with them because in a way, it confirms their worst fears. Women hear old clichés at work. "What's this business about being afraid of making us cry?" they ask. "How many times have you seen a woman cry at work?" Women hear men implying that all women are the same and that men can't afford to be direct with any of them.

The Insight for Women

Women aren't happy to hear that men really *do* treat them cautiously. But when men talk about how careful they feel they need to be with women, women see that what they thought was dismissive behavior is really hesitancy. This is one of the women's first "Ah-hah!" moments. They realize that when men seem to be brushing them off, they are really just being careful. And the reason they are being careful? They honestly don't know what the rules are. They don't know how women will react to what they say and do, and they are afraid to either offend or be misunderstood—or both. So men often act in ways that let them steer clear of problems, conflicts, and friction with women; they just try to find ways of avoiding these things. Women should understand that men's caution derives from concerns that are for them a big challenge. Once women recognize that reality, they can let men know they understand how the men feel and can assure them there is no need to be cautious because they are women.

The Insight for Men

Men see that when they hesitate with women, when they skirt around issues in order to avoid the challenges they confront, women feel they are being dismissed—and, quite naturally, the women react negatively. To solve this, men should just try being as direct as possible with women, even to the point of telling the women they are afraid of their reaction. Women will welcome this approach. To them, it will resonate as honest and considerate.

Challenge 2—Men Feel Confused

Men say:

✓ "I wish I knew the ground rules with women; do I call you 'women'? 'ladies'? 'girls'? 'guys'?"

✓ "Do I open the door for women or don't I?"

✓ "Is it okay to talk to women about their families at work?"

Most men work in a hierarchical "male" work paradigm, but the rules are changing, and men know it. That leaves them confused. Lots of men say they were brought up to show respect for women, but when this aspect of their upbringing comes to the surface, they get mixed signals from women. This leaves men wondering what they're supposed to do.

One young engineer told me the story of a scene he witnessed between two colleagues. "I watched this team from our office come out of the elevator after a tough meeting," he recalled. "A senior guy put his hand on one of the women's shoulders and congratulated her for her good work and she snapped back, 'From the elbow down please!' I mean, I was shocked that she would have that kind of reaction when the guy really meant well."

Over and over again, men report that

✓ They were brought up to be polite and considerate to women, but when that's how they behave, they get mixed signals back.

✓ What they learned from their mother, sister, or spouse doesn't seem to apply when it comes to their female colleagues.

✓ They want to help women out by, say, offering them a ride home, but they are afraid it will seem like they're coming on to them.

✓ They don't know how physical contact will be interpreted.

✓ They feel like they have to be on guard when it comes to dealing with women.

Women's Reaction

Women see that men's anxiety is real. They don't yet understand why men are so confused, but they do see that the confusion exists and is genuine. It's often a relief for women: they have always sensed men's uncertainty around them and wondered what was behind it.

Women don't understand that what men are telling them is that when it's "just men," everyone knows the norms and expectations and just follows the rules and procedures. Lots of men wonder whether these "men's rules" are still appropriate in the workplace, but among men, they work, and they supply men with a comfort zone.

Men say they don't spend a lot of time thinking about things like "how to deliver the message" to other men, while most women are unaware that the communication process becomes much more complicated for men when they're dealing with women. They get different reactions from different women in different situations—or even from the same woman at different times. That leaves men confused and desperately searching for a set of rules they can apply whenever they are dealing with women.

The Insight for Women

When men are confused about the rules of how to act with women, or how to communicate things to women, they often end up not saying what they mean for fear of being misunderstood. That solves one problem but creates another: it makes women feel excluded. When men act reluctant or hesitant, women feel as though they are being left out of the loop or pushed out of inner circles where decisions are being made. Women have to realize that this is not what was intended. For example, when asking questions, women should frame them in an open-ended and non-blaming way so that the men feel included. And, as we'll see later, being included is what women report as one of their main challenges in dealing with men!

The Insight for Men

There is no single set of rules for working with women. As soon as you start to apply a single set of rules, women will sense it—and they won't like it. Instead, men should try to deal with women as they would with a client—that is, with their antennae up, constantly aware, and looking for feedback. Engage, be interested, and ask for information. As you read on about women's challenges and better understand their perspective, it will become easier.

Challenge 3—Men Fear Being Accused of Harassment

Men say:

✓   "I won't even go to lunch with a woman anymore."

✓   "Do I ask her out for dinner when we are working late? No way."

✓   "I'm even worried when I'm alone in an elevator with a woman."

Although there are statistically more charges of employment discrimination than of harassment these days, men continue to be concerned about being accused of the latter; they are terrified of false allegations. As one man put it, "I've seen what one of my colleagues went through when he was accused of harassing a female colleague. I know for a fact he wasn't, but the company crucified him." Because of what they've seen happening around them, men are determined to do everything they can to avoid any accusations—to the point of not even commenting on a female colleague's new haircut. Men are afraid that since they don't know what the rules are, they could do something as a friendly gesture that women may misconstrue as harassment.

It's hard to overestimate the fear men have of being falsely accused of harassment. Men have seen it or heard about it and are convinced that there's nothing as career-limiting as being labeled a harasser. Even the suggestion that someone is *contemplating* bringing an action against them frightens men.

Women's Reaction

Women are always surprised to find out how worried men are about harassment. This may come as a surprise to men, but women don't actually spend a lot of time worrying about the possibility of harassment (unless, of course, they have actually been harassed, in which case it becomes a very real concern). Women say they had no idea that men felt this way, or that the men they thought they had built a good relationship with still shared this concern. As one woman put it, "To me it's pretty simple to see when it's harassment and when it's not."

The Insight for Women

Men's fear of harassment charges results in them holding back on relating to women, which women may assume shows that a man doesn't care or is disinterested or distant. But in fact, as women now see, men do care; they just don't know how to show it anymore. Women should understand the degree to which this fear is a concern—it's absolutely impossible to trivialize. There is no easy answer as to what women should do. You have to build relationships and build the level of trust so men feel safe.

The Insight for Men

Men are surprised to find out that women don't really spend much time thinking about harassment. My advice to them? Don't hold back in your relationships with women. Do your homework (as you would with a client) and think things through. Women will always welcome a well-framed compliment. But if you hold back too much, the fun and humor at the office will quickly disappear. And when that happens, everyone loses.

Challenge 4—Men Perceive Overt Focus on Women

Men say:

✓ "I see some job ads and just think that white males need not apply."

✓ "I think the best candidate should get the job, not the best woman candidate, but that doesn't seem to be the way the world works these days."

✓ "I saw a woman become vice president without any operational experience! Are you going to try to tell me it wasn't just because she's a woman?"

✓ "In hiring and promotion today, it's a numbers game, and women are benefiting disproportionately."

Some men believe that the white male is slipping further and further down the corporate ladder. Statistics may not support their feelings that white men are being systematically passed over for the best jobs, but individual and anecdotal experiences continue to feed their pessimism. Many men take a look at their future and conclude that because of equal employment opportunity policies, their options are limited.

The men who already have established careers don't feel they're free from the "preference" for women either. As one man told me, "There's all this stuff out there for women—networks and clubs for women only, special interest groups for professional women. If I belonged to a club for men only, people would say it was chauvinism."

On a closely related theme, many men bring up the problem of double standards that favor women, like male-bashing. "Women can joke about men now and it's considered perfectly acceptable," they tell me. There is also a feeling that men (and incidentally, women without children) are still expected to work harder than women with children. "Nobody questions it when a woman has to leave early to take care of her children, but I'm still expected to be there," one man told me.

Women's Reaction

Most women think the suggestion of an overt focus on women—a kind of reverse discrimination—is a myth. They know that some men believe that women are being promoted because they're women, that there's more attention on women in the workplace than on men, and that qualified men are being overlooked because of this. But this doesn't cut any ice with women—particularly the women who work in nontraditional fields and constantly feel that they have to struggle to get taken seriously.

The Insight for Women

I encourage them to put these feelings aside when they listen to men talk about reverse discrimination. Many men do genuinely feel that there is overt attention to women and that this works against them. And that perception affects men's behavior toward women. Whether, statistically, the focus on women exists, or is justified if it does, is not the point. When men feel reverse discrimination, they react with cynicism and a kind of defeatist attitude. The feeling is this: "She'll get the job anyway, because she's a woman. So why should

I bother?" They're only talking about their own feelings, but the inadvertent result is to reinforce one of women's Top Challenges: the fear of being a "token." This reaction, in turn, feeds women's feeling that they are being tested all the time.

Again, recognize that men's perception is real for them. Women should challenge men to validate their perceptions. Ask for specific statistics that their perception is a reality, and soon men will see that it's not a reality but a myth. Show them the numbers, but be careful not to blame individual men for their perceptions.

The Insight for Men

Although equal employment opportunity policies are a reality, reverse discrimination is a myth. Men should avoid generalizing; one scenario of a woman who moved up a few levels too quickly does not a trend make. What these policies have done is force employers to be more objective in their decisions. They have to justify their choices now. Traditionally, men have been employed for their potential, while women tended to be employed for their track record and proven skills. Equal opportunity means everyone has to be employed according to the same criteria.

Challenge 5—Men Feel Blamed

Men say:

✓ "When I hear the words 'male-dominated workplace,' it just sounds like feminist male-bashing to me."

✓ "Why do women blame all men for the historical mistakes of a few?"

✓ "I feel like I have to apologize for being a man these days."

Many men feel they have been painted with the same wide brush—an image created, they believe, by an extremist feminist movement—and that women lump them together as a group. "We're never treated as individuals," men tell me. "Just because your boss mistreated you 15 years ago doesn't mean it's my fault." Every time they hear the words "male-dominated," they feel as if they're being blamed for something they had no control over. "I feel blamed for breathing," some have told me.

Women's Reaction

Here, the lights really start going on for women. Most women have witnessed, participated in, or initiated some male-bashing at work, and they know it. In a world where the power balance has traditionally favored men, women feel justified in such behavior. It seems normal, even acceptable these days to take a stab at men, all in good humor. Some women, particularly the older ones, even make jokes when men present this challenge. "But you ARE wrong!" they say.

But when women see that comments like these strike men as a major challenge—and a serious injustice—it becomes clear to them that their joking attitude is not harmless fun. They see that even if they consider the behavior innocuous and acceptable, men don't. Men feel blamed for being men. Women are always surprised to find this out. What women consider a sort of teasing equates to men as "blaming me for breathing." There's a glimmer of light appearing, however, as women step out of their shoes and start to look at their own behavior from a man's perspective.

The Insight for Women

When men feel they are being painted with that same brush, they often react, without even realizing it, with a dismissive or even cynical behavior toward women. Women hear the message. It reinforces some of their top challenges, as you will see in the next chapter: the feelings of being dismissed, excluded, and tested. Nevertheless, women should avoid making sweeping generalizations about men; avoid saying "all men are," and treat men as individuals that are at different Stages of Awareness.

The Insight for Men

Women do have a tendency to see patterns and to speak globally about men when they feel they are victims of discrimination, but men should take a stand on this one and challenge women they feel are blaming them, unfairly, for being men. (Of course, men must take care not to unfairly blame women in return!)

It might be interesting for both male and female readers to know that the "challenges" men and women present are almost always the same all over the world. Year after year, men always say the same things about working with women, and women say the same things about working with men. It doesn't matter if they are lawyers or accountants, secretaries or soldiers, middle managers, chief executive officers, office workers, middle-aged or thirty-something. The same themes come up, over and over again.

So, where men are concerned, is it true? Are the new rules really working against men? The only "truth" I'm really interested in is men's perceptions and how those perceptions affect their interactions with women. After listening to thousands of men talk about what it feels like to work with women, I can say with absolute certainty that they really do feel this way. Men really are confused, they really do feel they have to be cautious when they're dealing with women, they perceive that they are being unfairly blamed for the way chauvinists have acted in the past, and they honestly feel that they are paying the price by being victims of what they see as an undue focus on women and reverse discrimination against men. Women might not like what they hear, but they have to accept that it is an accurate picture of how many men feel. And of course, women should listen to men—because men's challenges shed light on a lot of the behavior that women can misinterpret.

———

What you've read in this chapter are the distilled perceptions voiced by tens of thousands of men about what it feels like to work with women: what worries them, what confuses them, and what leaves them perplexed. This is not about who's right and who's wrong. You'll soon see why.

No doubt these perceptions have left the women reading them wondering, "Then what should I do?" Read on. The answers are ahead.

But first, women, it's your turn to talk. And men, it's time for you to listen.

5

The Word to Men: "Attention Must Be Paid" to Your Women Colleagues

The mind, once stretched by a new insight, never regains its original dimensions.

—O.W. Holmes, "The Poet at the Breakfast Table"

I started the chapter on men's challenges with a warning for women to avoid judging men too quickly. "Look for insights," I advised. When women really listen to men talking about their challenges working with women, they are often surprised—even amazed—by what they hear.

This chapter starts with a similar warning to men: try to resist arguing with what the women say. Your tendency will likely be to regard the stories that illustrate the women's challenges as isolated incidents. That makes it easy to assume that each story "only happened that one time," and therefore "it didn't mean anything." Particularizing each point is a way of challenging what women say, rather than trying to understand women's point of view.

Well, men, the fact of the matter is, when women talk about their challenges, while each may relate an individual incident, that incident is only one illustration of their discouragement over the build-up of similar incidents. The drip, drip, drip effect of repeated experiences has become a kind of water torture that really gets to women, and while women may realize that a man's behavior is not necessarily congruent with his intentions, that does not seem to have slowed the cascade.

A woman's boss calls her "sweetie" or "dear." The press called British Prime Minister Tony Blair's senior female colleagues "Blair

Babes." U.S. President George W. Bush called his senior female colleagues "My Moms." No one of these diminutive "nicknames" may be a big deal on its own, but when you've heard something like them continually from different male colleagues over the years, it starts to wear you down. It's easy for men to particularize and challenge these kinds of complaints, but women have heard it all before, and it has grown stale.

My advice to men on this issue is the same as my advice to women. Forget about who's right and who's wrong. Resist the temptation to disprove what the opposite gender is saying. Put aside your opinions, your well-worn ideas, and the judgments you've formed based on past experiences, and look instead for those "Ah-hah" moments that tell you you're learning something new. I've heard women say the same things and raise the same complaints over and over again, from year to year, from profession to profession. There's got to be something in it.

And finally, men, remember that you are getting a rare opportunity to go behind closed doors and listen to what women say when you're not around. You're about to hear how women feel at work. Consider this an opportunity to put yourself in women's shoes.

Women's Top Five Challenges Working with Men

Interestingly, when I ask women about the challenges they experience working with men, there are always a few women who put up their hands and declare, "There's no difference between women and men." According to these women, problems at work aren't because of gender—"gender has nothing to do with it"—but are due to "individual personalities." Curiously, it's usually the younger women who make these claims. When the older women hear this, they often nod their heads and say, "You just haven't been working with men long enough. You'll see."

That odd exception aside, however, most women have plenty to say about what it feels like to work with men. It's as if women have been harboring these thoughts for years but have never had the chance to voice them. There is no dead air in the women's room. And that's not the only difference from the men's room. While the men tend to challenge each other until they decide who's right, women always treat the brainstorming session as a team effort. They instinctively turn the exercise into a collaborative process, sharing experiences with one another and building on them. At first, as the women start to talk, a chorus of recognition takes over the room; "uh-huhs" are heard from nodding heads, and soon all the women are reinforcing each other's experience with their own, effectively building a list. It's not unusual for women to come up with ten or twelve pages of challenges on their flipchart, while men usually come up with only one or two.

One thing that still surprises me about women is how shocked so many of them are to find out that other women share their feelings about working with men. Amazing as it sounds, women may talk a lot together about the men they work with, but they rarely share their deepest personal feelings about the subject. It's easy to talk about what men are and how men act, but it's harder to talk about how their behavior makes you feel. Women, think back to the many times you've talked to your female colleagues about men, and you'll see this is probably true for you, too. Women rarely talk together about how men's behavior affects them—particularly as they rise through the ranks and have to be more cautious about revealing the problems they may be experiencing.

Why do so many women keep their real feelings to themselves? Strangely, it's because deep down, they worry the feelings spring from an inadequacy on their part. It all boils down to the way many women internalize the problems they experience at work, looking for the answers to the problems in their own behavior—something women do all the time. They may tell other women about a problem with a particular man, but instinctively, women wonder whether *they themselves* played a role in creating the problem. It's very subtle. Most women don't know they're doing it.

So when women hear other women articulate exactly what they've been thinking for years, their faces light up. Your face will probably light up too as you hear from the women in the women's room in the pages that follow. After living through decades of gender-based miscommunications wondering, "What's wrong with me?" they are amazed when they at last learn that other women struggle with the same problems and feel exactly the same way they do about working with men.

And as with the men, our workshop is often the first formal opportunity women have had to speak openly about what it's like to work with the other gender. Here are some of the challenges they articulate. If you are a woman, feel free to tick off those you relate to.

✓   Women feel dismissed.

✓   Women feel excluded.

✓   Women feel scrutinized.

✓   Women feel they have to act like men.

✓   Women are concerned about tokenism.

Challenge 1—Women Feel Dismissed

Women say:

✓   "Men don't seek my opinion, or if they do, they ignore it."

✓   "Men talk a lot, but they don't listen."

✓   "My boss doesn't include me in the conversation!"

Women often feel their words somehow don't have the same weight as the words spoken by their male counterparts. Many women tell about experiences at meetings where they made an important point or came up with a new idea only to have it ignored. But when the same point was later picked up by a male coworker, everyone listened. "Men seem to listen only to men, no matter what we say," they tell me. When these women try to explore an issue by talking about various aspects of a problem, they feel that men shut them off, and that they are being dismissed and discounted.

Many women also feel that old stereotypes about women are preventing men from listening to them. "When I bring up ideas and remind my male colleagues of past discussions, they tell me I'm 'nagging,'" says one woman.

Women say:

- ✓ "When we make points at meetings, we get passed over. Then a man takes the point up and says more or less the same thing and everyone gives him three cheers. It's as though we're not there."
- ✓ "When I try to talk through problems at work I just get grunts from men. It's as though men just want to get to the bottom line and get on to something else, as fast as possible."
- ✓ "When I bring up sensitive issues, no one listens to me. If I continue to raise the issues, I'm accused of being irritating. What would be praised as persistence in a man becomes a negative when a woman does it."
- ✓ "The tone changes when I enter a room full of men. Their behavior changes, their body language shifts, their language alters, and the mood is different."

Men's Reaction

When they hear women say they feel dismissed, men's first reaction is to map women's feelings onto their own experience. The inevitable conclusion is "Sometimes I feel dismissed, too. So what?" They usually pursue this line of reasoning by challenging women, picking apart the examples women have given, and asking for more proof.

The Insight for Men

What usually happens is this: as the men continue to argue over whether women's complaints are legitimate or not, somebody in the room finally gets it. "Listen, guys," he will say. "Look at us; we're doing exactly what the women say we do: we're arguing among ourselves so nobody can get a word in edgewise. *Maybe we do dismiss them!*"

Typically, for men, this is their first "Ah-hah" moment, but it's the one that becomes a summons to men to listen actively to women, and even when they feel women may be digressing from "the point," to concede that what they're saying may be relevant. Men, if you find that a woman's train of thought follows a different track from the one you're used to, think again about what you've heard as you try to clarify what was said on its own terms.

The Insight for Women

Men aren't the only ones who have an "Ah-hah" here. Many women also realize that the fear of being dismissed changes their behavior, too. Because women are on the defensive when they go into meetings, they unknowingly send a message to men to be careful. Then what happens? Men often react to that signal, without even thinking about it, by pulling back and becoming cautious—one of men's top challenges working with women. Women have to realize that men's behavior is not intentional and that men are not deliberately dismissing them.

Challenge 2—Women Feel Excluded

Women say:

- ✓ "I always feel the real meeting takes place after the meeting, when the men go out for a drink."
- ✓ "I just don't seem to be able to get into the real corridors of power, no matter how hard I try."
- ✓ "Men use sports or war talk to describe strategies. I can't use that kind of language, so I feel I can't make my voice heard."

It doesn't matter whether I'm talking to female lawyers, accountants, police officers, or sales people. Most women in business have been in a similar situation and have been left with more or less the same feeling. A woman comes to a table where men are gathered around, often talking about sports. She tries to fit into the conversation and even cracks a few jokes, but the men just take a look at her and carry on talking to each other. For a woman, it feels as though the men are deliberately ignoring her. Women already feel they have to struggle to be part of the team, but the cold-shoulder treatment only confirms to them that no matter what they do, they will always be excluded just because they are women.

The famous "meeting after the meeting" also serves to alienate female colleagues. You know how it works: a group of men goes out for a beer after work. They don't invite their female colleague; maybe they assume she won't be interested, or maybe they just don't even think about her. How does she feel? As if the real meetings take place after hours and she's shut out of them. So she feels she's deliberately excluded from the decision-making process.

If the woman is invited to attend the gathering, another dynamic sets in. When she arrives, the men are talking about football, golf, last night's hockey game, or tonight's basketball thriller. Maybe she's interested, maybe she's not, but it doesn't matter. The men will be having fun, teasing one another, taking jabs at each other—typical male banter. Women feel this bonding going on between men. They don't want to be part of the locker-room talk, but, again, they do feel excluded by it.

Women say:

✓ They never know how to "get on the inside."

✓ They are not invited along with "the guys," or they are actually told by their male colleagues, "Believe me, you wouldn't want to come."

✓ Their male colleagues "congregate in a male colleague's office, sit around with other men, the boss included." To women, it looks as if it just kind of happens naturally, and they aren't included.

Men's Reaction

Men's first reaction is typically that they too sometimes feel excluded. That misses the point that women feel they're being excluded because they're *women*. Our workshop's male facilitator often takes this opportunity to jump into the discussion. "Imagine," he'll suggest, "that the feeling you've experienced once or twice of being left out of a decision were to happen *every day of your working life*. Imagine you can see it coming when you walk into a boardroom meeting. Imagine it as a daily pattern. No matter how good you are, you're never invited to the important meetings. Lots of your women colleagues feel this way all the time."

The Insight for Men

The clarification usually works, especially if it is reinforced by a male member of a racial or ethnic minority affirming that it's a feeling he can relate to. His colleagues then see the light; it isn't about specific examples but a recurring pattern: the water-torture drip.

Understand that that's what this experience is for women—sheer torture. Make sure that you introduce your female colleagues in a powerful and credible way in meetings with your clients, making sure you acknowledge their skills and talents. This will go a long way toward eliminating this challenge women so often confront.

The Insight for Women

Again, when women hear men's reaction, they often start putting two and two together and seeing a kernel of truth in it. The fear of being excluded, like the fear of being dismissed, often puts women on the defensive. Women are so accustomed to feeling excluded, in fact, that they are not even aware of their defensiveness. Reminded of it in the workshop, they realize that it changes their behavior, goading them to act more aggressively or more brashly than they normally would.

Men pick up that signal. They don't necessarily understand it; they just react to it. How? Again, by pulling back—by being more cautious and more careful. And that reaction, in turn, reinforces women's feeling that they are being excluded.

Women would do well to be more proactive in dealing with this situation. Look for ways to collaborate. Invite yourself in. And men, remember: women *do* want to be invited in.

Challenge 3—Women Feel Tested

Women say:

✓ "With my clients, but even sometimes with my colleagues, it always feels as though there's this assumption that women just don't have what it takes."

✓ "I think women are scrutinized more than men—even by other women!"

✓ "I feel I get questioned on my knowledge of technical aspects of my work a lot more than the men I work with do. People take it for granted that a man knows what he's talking about, but they wonder about a woman."

Many women believe that they have to work harder than their male colleagues in order to prove themselves. "I can only prove myself by sheer accomplishment, by being indisputably good," they tell me. They constantly feel that their male colleagues are testing them, doubting their capabilities. They feel as though there's a different set of standards for women.

The feeling that you are assumed to be inferior can easily undermine your self-confidence. It's as if everything—even the way you dress or groom yourself—has the potential to lower your credibility. Some executive women say that they would never walk around in casual clothes on casual Fridays; they're afraid it would undermine their authority. In fields where technical ability is essential, many women feel that their peers and their clients constantly doubt their competency. The more traditionally male-dominated the field of work, the more the women feel they have to meet higher standards than men do to get the same respect.

Women say:

✓ "Men get promoted for their potential, but women get promoted if they can demonstrate what they have already accomplished."

✓ "It feels as if there's an ongoing assumption that we have inferior skills or that we don't have as much technical ability as a man in the same position would."

✓ "There's an unspoken question: 'Does she know her stuff?'"

✓ "Men get credibility simply by doing their job, but women have to earn it. It's as if women have a different starting point."

Men's Reaction

A lot of men own up to the validity of these feelings on the part of their female colleagues. Many admit that they have more confidence dealing with other men, especially if it's a first-time meeting. This is salt in women's wounds. The issue is particularly sensitive in organizations where women don't have a strong presence: the police, the armed forces, traditional trades, even among litigation lawyers. Yet for men, the conversation triggers their fear of being blamed. They have a hard time extracting themselves from the issue enough to hear women's words for what they are: an authentic expression of how it feels to work with men. Fortunately, there are often men present who have gone out on a limb to promote women. "When you push for women, it works," they say.

The Insight for Men

Because women tend to go to work with the feeling that they are being tested, they often feel they have to work harder, perform better, and generally do more than their male colleagues to get the same recognition. Men notice this, but they jump to the wrong conclusions, perceiving it as the women lacking confidence and feeling, for some reason, that they have to prove themselves. Well, it's not that women lack confidence. Women feel they are always being tested and therefore that they really do have something to prove.

And there's more. Women pick up on men's feeling that they lack confidence. This makes them feel even more tested.

The Insight for Women

Women can avoid setting off this self-perpetuating cycle of feeling tested by establishing their credibility right at the start. Don't wait for anyone to doubt you. Introducing yourself in a straightforward manner, explaining who you are, what you do, and what your background is, will do the trick.

Challenge 4—Aping the Clichés of Alpha-Male Behavior

Women say:

✓ "If I want to be taken seriously, I have to fit in. I have to be more forceful and more aggressive. I can't really afford to be myself."

✓ "I don't really like being so hard, so tough and distant, and directing people the way I do. The problem is, it works!"

✓ "Sometimes I think my family would never recognize me if they saw me at work."

When you've been in the workforce for, say, a decade, during which time you have felt ignored, dismissed, and excluded, your behavior does start to change. Many women concede that they have become "more assertive and forceful"; they have aped the apes, taking on the storied clichés connected with the behavior of dominant alpha-male animals in the wild. It may mean they try out inauthentic behavior, affect an aggressiveness they don't possess, or raise their voice for effect.

But there's a price to pay for this attempt at domineering behavior. Although you may get respect, you may also find that neither women nor men will be comfortable working with you as, step by step, you give up who you are to create what you believe to be a "professional" persona. Behind your back, they'll be calling you names—steamroller, dragon lady, or worse—or dubbing you "Miranda Priestly," the fictional, cold-fish magazine editor of *The Devil Wears Prada*. "I worked so hard to just be a straight, no-nonsense worker," one very senior executive woman told me, "and now I just get called a barracuda."

Men's Reaction

When a woman takes on this kind of autocratic behavior in order to show her mettle, it often makes men steer as far away from her as possible. Here's how our workshop's male co-facilitator explains it to these men: "Imagine wearing a suit of armor to work every day. Imagine having to act as though you're someone else every working day, just to have the feeling that you're being taken seriously. That's why she acts like a steamroller."

Some of the women in the room admit that they've changed so much and for so long that they're not sure they could give up their authoritarian behavior. Some of them don't think they would want to give it up. Why not? Because it works.

(This insight reminds some men in the room of a tone of voice they were surprised to hear their wives assume on the phone with a colleague or client. Aha! It was her "work" personality coming through!)

The Insight for Men

Men need to understand that most women don't choose to steam-roll over colleagues or bite like barracudas. They feel they have no alternative if they are going to have a chance of succeeding in an atmosphere in which only such behavior gets them noticed.

The Insight for Women

The problem with taking on this clichéd sort of behavior is the consequences that invariably result. First, such behavior leaves men colleagues more confused. They feel blamed, and they then act more carefully than ever. And of course, when men pull back and act carefully, that ends up making women feel as though they have to steam-roll even harder in order to get respect! There's a real cost associated with this kind of behavior—not just to colleagues, but to the women themselves. Trying to influence rather than dominate people is a much better way to earn respect.

Challenge 5—Women Feel Like Tokens

Women say:

✓ "Men always think I got this promotion because I'm a woman."
✓ "I didn't want preferential treatment. I just wanted the job I deserved!"
✓ "I feel as if there is a price for getting this promotion. I'm under the microscope all the time!"

Many women tend to look at the workplace and see a no-win situation. When they are hired, they feel that men are suspicious about how they got the job. Programs to promote women add to this problem, as the perception is that a quota rather than a set of qualifications is the determining factor for women rising in the hierarchy. It adds to a woman's burden to feel that her colleagues suspect she got the job or promotion because of her gender. She feels she enters the job under a magnifying glass, and if she makes a mistake, it will be attributed to the fact that she is female. It's like carrying the weight of the world on your shoulders.

Men's Reaction

When women talk about how it feels to be viewed as tokens, men usually react by saying, "Yes, but we're victims of reverse discrimination, so it all evens out." Yet there's another, equally important aspect to this particular women's challenge, and our workshops encourage men to see it—namely, it is the mirror image of the challenge men articulated about an undue focus on women. If men can see their resentment of so-called preferential treatment for women mirrored in women's fears of being regarded as a "token" and having to adapt to that role, we just may be able to narrow the gap between men and women and make it possible for them to work together effectively.

The Insight for Men

Although men react defensively at first, they eventually come to see that workplace policies to promote women do not guarantee women an easy time on the job—the proverbial "walk in the park." Those very policies add to women's feeling that they are being tested. And how do women respond? They feel that they have to work harder. They try to prove men wrong before they're ever accused of anything.

Men often claim that the women they work with overcompensate, or work too hard, or are too perfectionist. Now they get a clue as to why women act that way. It's not because women are insecure. It's because women feel tested.

For most men, achieving this insight definitely constitutes an "Ah-hah" moment.

The Insight for Women

It's tough for women to feel good about their work when they fear they got their job because the Human Resources department needed to adjust some numbers. It's not an empowering feeling to carry around with you. And it ends up reinforcing women's feeling of being tested and of having to prove something. We've already seen what this does to women. The feeling of being a token makes women act defensively, it can make them feel they have to overcompensate, and it can sometimes prod them to be more aggressive than they would normally be. They react to feeling like a token by working harder. But unfortunately, men often think this is a sign that women lack confidence.

My advice to women? Don't let yourselves fall into the trap of feeling tested. Develop a network of support around you. Don't try to bear the burden of proving women can do the job all alone.

———

By this point in this book, both men and women readers have had the golden opportunity to stand in the other gender's shoes. You've each heard what the opposite sex has to say about working with you and you've seen how your own behavior feeds those challenges.

It's time now to do something to improve the situation. In the next three chapters, you'll see how men and women speak different languages, hear different stories, and see different worlds. And you'll see what you can do to bridge the gap between those worlds.

6

Same Words, Different Language

Our conversational styles are different. If what you're after is not just self-expression but communication—then it's not enough for the language to be right; it must be understood.

—Deborah Tannen, Professor of Linguistics,
You Just Don't Understand

So we've seen that men and women think differently. We process information differently. But we still speak the same language—don't we? Surely we can solve our problems just by talking.

Actually, talking isn't the complete solution. Sometimes, talking is part of the problem. This is because men and women don't just think and process information differently; we also communicate differently. Even when we use the same words, we often don't mean the same thing. Most of us have an intuitive sense of this, but we don't think about it much. We just carry on assuming that the other gender means the same thing we mean and interprets things the same way we do. We listen to the other gender from our own frame of reference. And we have already seen what kinds of misinterpretations that can lead to.

Without gender awareness, language can hamper or befuddle communication. Men and women often don't mean the same things when they use the same words. They often don't hear the same words the same way. So what happens? When we communicate, we assume the other gender means the same thing we do and hears the same way we do. Then we evaluate their reactions from that standpoint. We read our meanings into what they say and do. We don't stop for a second to wonder if the opposite gender might just be looking at things completely differently. Instead, we jump to conclusions. Or worse, we miss the message entirely.

75

From Denmark

other cultures

I learned a lesson very early in life about how people can think differently and about the kinds of mistakes I could make by assuming people thought the same way I did. I left my native Denmark at a young age when I got married and moved to Italy. Very few cultures could be as different as those of Copenhagen and Rome. In Denmark, I had grown up in a world where people on the whole were calm, polite, and reserved. Danes are very careful not to offend, not to be seen to observe others' behavior, not to take too much "air time." They have a highly developed sense of what's appropriate and believe in good manners.

Imagine how I felt when I arrived in Rome with these ideas. When I suddenly found myself immersed in Italian culture, I thought this:

✓ Why are the Italians so angry all the time?

✓ They're constantly fighting!

✓ They're so loud! Why can't they be quiet?

It's not hard to see my mistake. I was mapping Italian behavior onto my Danish frame of reference. For the Danish, loudness signals anger, fighting signals a breakdown, and noise is to be avoided. But not for Italians. What a mistake I was making! Slowly, as I got to know Italian culture better and mastered the language, my perspective changed and I started to see Italians from within their own frame of reference. After about three months in Italy, I had to throw all my assumptions out the window. I remember how my thinking changed. I realized this:

It would be better if men and women spoke different languages

✓ They're not angry. They're passionate!

✓ They're not fighting. They love to use their beautiful language to debate with one another.

✓ They're not interfering in other people's business. They're being open with each other. They ask about each other's problems because they care and bond that way!

I've often said that men and women would be better off if they actually didn't speak the same language. Maybe then we wouldn't take so many things for granted. We would pay more attention to how we say things and how the other gender interprets what we say. We would try to put ourselves in the other's shoes. We would test out ideas from another perspective. We would stop and think that maybe a certain word or gesture or way of arguing doesn't mean the same thing for men as it does for women. We wouldn't take it for granted that the other gender understands our words, and we'd make an extra effort to ensure that they do.

Are men and women really so foreign to each other? The ones who attend my workshops certainly believe it after they've done the following "communications" quiz. It is a list of common, everyday words and phrases. I ask men and women to write down what they mean. You might want to try it yourself before you read what men and women each say.

As you'll see, men and women have quite different ideas about the meaning of words that we all use every day. Imagine the confusion and frustration this creates. Not only do men and women understand the same words differently, they also jump to conclusions about what certain types of reaction mean when they come from the other gender. Luckily, there are solutions.

Before I tell you how differently men and women interpret some common words and phrases, please complete the following quiz:

Language Quiz

Obviously, men should please complete the section under **He**, and women should please complete the section under **She**. Now if you think that you might have the other gender figured out, I invite you to stand in their shoes and complete their sentences.

How Men and Women Listen

Yes!

    HE: What I mean when I say "Yes!" is ____*yes*____.
    SHE: What I mean when I say "Yes!" is ____*maybe*____.

What do you think?

    HE: I'm being asked to ____*choose one*____.
    SHE: I'm being asked to ____*talk it through*____.

What's the value of building a team?

HE: I would build a team to ___*make something*___.

SHE: I would build a team to ___*network*___.

How do you present an idea?

HE: I would say ___*heres my idea*___.

SHE: I would say ___*what do you think*___.

How do you argue effectively?

HE: My approach would be to ___*what am I arguing for*___.

SHE: My approach would be to ___*lay it all out*___.

What is success at work?

HE: I experience success at work when ___*I complete things*___.

SHE: I experience success at work when ___*we complete things*___.

How do you listen effectively?

HE: My approach would be to ___*be quiet an listen*___.

SHE: My approach would be to ___*ask questions*___.

Now that you've answered this quiz, you'll get the opportunity to compare your answers with those of thousands of men and women. And when you see how differently men and women look at these statements, you'll see how those differences create misunderstandings, and you'll learn how to prevent them.

"Yes"

What Men Hear

"I agree. That's final. Let's move on."

What Women Hear

"I'm listening. I may not agree, but I'm tracking."

The Misunderstanding

For men, "Yes" is the destination. When you've arrived there, there's nothing more to say. For women, "Yes" means the trip has started. For women, "Yes" is not definitive. It means there is something going on. It's a word they associate with a *process*, not an *answer*.

Imagine the number of problems this simple but essential word can cause. Imagine what happens when men hear a woman say "Yes." They assume she means what they mean, yet they then see her react in a way that doesn't fit that picture. "You never know when yes means yes with a woman," men tell me.

Yet imagine how women feel when they hear men say "Yes." They interpret it as an invitation to keep fleshing out a topic, and they then find out the case has been closed. This misunderstanding causes confusion and leads to frustration—or worse. And it ends up reinforcing assumptions men and women already have about each other.

One man gave me the following example: "I was on my way to a meeting and discussed my idea with a female colleague. She said, 'Yes.' But when we got to the meeting she turned around and started suggesting revisions." He felt attacked and ambushed. "I couldn't believe it! I thought I had her on my side! What on earth does 'yes' mean if it doesn't mean you agree?"

What do men conclude from these kinds of misunderstanding? That women are shifty, that you can never tell what a woman means. And how do they react? By being careful. It's men's number one challenge working with women, and that's why. It's a basic misunderstanding based on gender difference.

When a man abruptly closes a discussion with a "Yes," and a woman thinks the discussion is just getting started, the woman feels dismissed. Women also sense it when men are being careful. "Men are not really listening. Men are avoiding and dismissing us," women say.

There is, of course, a cultural factor that exacerbates this whole situation. Women on the whole are brought up to be polite. One of the ways we're taught to be polite is to avoid saying "No" outright. I remember a period in my days as a sales executive when I tried to unlearn that habit. Like many women, I have a tendency to avoid a flat "No" by explaining my way around a negative reaction. But I felt this behavior was becoming a professional handicap. I sensed that people found me indecisive. So I practiced saying "No" without giving any explanation.

Of course it didn't work. I haven't changed. And why should I? It's futile for women to try to change their style. And it's futile for men to change theirs. So what should we do?

The Solution

For Both Men and Women

The solution is to understand what the other means by "Yes" and anticipate the misunderstandings that might come about without such understanding. I suggest a simple technique I call "Framing and Checking."

For Men

Check what kind of "Yes" you're getting. Is it "Yes, that's final," or "Yes, I'm following you, but let's explore this a little more"? Then tell women what kind of "Yes" you need. If you tell a woman you need a final answer, she won't feel she's being brushed off if you aren't open to more discussion.

For Women

Frame your "Yes" with some more information so men know what kind of yes they're getting. Tell them, "Yes. I'm listening." or "Yes, I see where you're coming from, but I need to talk about it more."

"What Do You Think?"

What Men Hear

Men hear the question as a call to action. They feel they are being challenged to take a position or make a statement or deliver a decision. So when they answer, they try to deliver something definitive. They give their best bottom line.

What Women Hear

Women hear the question as an invitation to talk about an issue, to express their thoughts and feelings. For women, it's not a one-way street. When someone says, "What do you think?" women hear "Let's discuss this." They try to initiate idea sharing. For women, giving an opinion is often not as important as getting a discussion going; the whole process counts. Women will wait for the discussion to progress until they arrive at what they see as the most effective time for them to express their feelings on the topic.

The Misunderstanding

Lets talk about it - indecisiveness, men making a decision - women sees as cold + dismissive

The potential for misinterpretation here is great. When women react to the question by opening the discussion, men interpret that as "She hasn't done her homework," or "She hasn't thought it through." They think, "Don't waste my time! Just give me the bottom line!" Men will see women's indecisiveness as a sign they lack confidence.

When men answer the question "What do you think?" with a definitive statement and then move on to the next issue, women feel they're being shut out. Women think, "I don't want a decision. I want to hear what you think." They often feel men are being cold and distant when they give categorical answers to questions, or that they are dismissing them. As one woman told me, "It's as if men don't think I can make up my own mind about things. When I ask for an opinion they give me answers and solutions. But I'm not asking them to solve my problems for me!"

men details - No

When women initiate idea sharing and ask for input, it's a way of being thorough. It makes them feel that they're doing their job well. Many women instinctively fear that in rushing to a conclusion, something may get overlooked. Most men want to agree on solutions and implement them. They want to be spared the details because the details get in the way of them doing their job.

Many women also feel that building good relationships makes people work better. Asking for someone's opinion is sometimes as much a way to build rapport as it is to get an answer. When men react in a way that makes women feel shut out, women are hurt and feel dismissed. After all, they were extending an invitation to solidify a relationship.

The Solution

For Men — to ask for clarity

When women ask, "What do you think?" check the question by asking, "Do you want exploration or do you want a definitive answer?" When men ask the question, it's wise to frame it. Ask, "What's your considered opinion on this matter? Do you think this is good or bad?"

For Women — to specifically ask for thier opinion

When women really want to know how men feel, they have to tell them so specifically. They can preface the question, "What do you think?" with a sentence like, "I have a clear opinion, but I want to explore your thoughts first," or, "I'm brainstorming. I really want us to take a good look at this problem and explore some possible solutions."

"Teamwork"

What Men Hear — Get a job done

For men, teams are primarily a means to an end. The use of teams is to get the job done. If men think they can do a job on their own, they won't bother with a team.

What Women Hear — Networking

For women, teams are more than a means to an end. They are also an opportunity. To do what? To build relationships and long-term support bases for other projects. Women may not keep a specific team together after the job has been completed, but they hope the relationships built among team members will continue.

The Misunderstanding

Since men see a team as the way to achieve a specific purpose, they tend to consider teams as temporary and finite. Since women see teamwork as an end in itself, they think of themselves as engaging in a long-term, ongoing process when they build teams.

The misunderstandings between men and women are predictable. Men tend to disband a team when the work is done and women want to use the team as the base for further collaboration. "We had a winning formula," women say. "We had really started something. Why would we throw that away just because we finished the job?"

Men usually see building rapport as a frill. "We're already pressed for time. Let's just get down to the task at hand," they say. But women think the team will be more effective if there is good rapport among the members. Without realizing it, men can make women feel as if all their valuable work is being tossed out the window, as though their work isn't appreciated and they therefore aren't valued.

The Solution

For Both Men and Women

Team building is one area where all businesses and organizations need to recognize women's and men's distinct strengths and try to put both to use. Teams do work better when the members share a common purpose and bond together toward that purpose. The rapport that is created through the team can be a useful resource to be drawn on even after the team has achieved its immediate purpose. But, of course, for the team to achieve its goals there must be a determination for action. Women need to appreciate the value of men's linear, goal-oriented approach, and men need to appreciate the value of women's skill for achieving rapport. Put these qualities together, and you will have a winning team.

"Tabling an Idea"

*[handwritten: Women - Start of convo
Men - Presenting a finished idea plan.]*

What Men Do

For men, tabling an idea means presenting a finished product and clearly stating a plan.

What Women Do

For women, tabling an idea means the beginning of a conversation. The objective is to get suggestions and input, not just state a plan. Women see it as a way to get a dialogue going.

The Misunderstanding

Here's a typical scenario of how women see it when they feel dismissed by men: "I state an idea. Everyone ignores me and then a man restates it and everyone loves it!" "Tabling an idea" is the classic situation where this happens. Women think the objective is to get the dialogue going. They try to be inclusive of everyone's opinions and to encourage collaboration. But when they do this, men think women are uncertain, unprepared, or unconvinced. They therefore reframe a woman's idea to clarify what was meant, to nail it down.

This situation leaves women feeling that their intentions have been misinterpreted and men feeling bewildered. As one man explained, "One of my female colleagues didn't seem convinced of an idea she put forward at a meeting. I thought it was a great idea. I restated it to support her. And her reaction was that I stole her idea! I don't get it." Women's inclusive style comes across to men as hesitancy. Men conclude that women lack confidence. When men state rather than suggest ideas, women feel the men aren't interested in their opinions. Their conclusion? "Men are so controlling."

The Solution

For Men

Men can make it clear that they are open to others' input by saying, "This is my idea. I think it's good, but it can always be better. I'm open to suggestions for improvement." They can also improve the "paraphrasing" scenario by asserting, for example, that "Amy had a great idea, but I'm not sure everyone heard it."

For Women

Women can avoid feeling that their ideas are stolen with a simple strategy—by asserting they've thought an idea through and are clear on what they want to do but seek further input from others. By stating their intentions this way, women "frame" their ownership of an idea.

"Arguments"

What Men Hear

Men think arguments are debates confined to the single issue at hand. They don't have anything to do with what happened in the past.

What Women Hear

Women think arguments encompass a person's character across a spectrum of faults. Women see a pattern, and that's what the argument is about. Women see signs of a person's character in what they say, and the arguments become about that, too.

The Misunderstanding

Women are acutely aware of patterns. Men will see a conflict stemming from specific circumstances, but women will immediately match that up to similar incidents or even similar arguments from the past. If a woman saw certain character flaws as responsible for a past situation, she will see them at work in the present situation as well.

When women see a person acting a certain way, they tend to attribute it to his or her character. A man will say, "He's behaving like an idiot." A woman will say, "He is an idiot."

Women do this because of the way they collect memories. Remember from Chapter 3 how interconnected women's brains are? Women remember not only what happened, but also how they experienced an event. And they connect a past feeling to a similar one in the present very quickly.

The men I talk to say they find women's "linking" behavior extremely frustrating. They think women are keeping scorecards. Some men feel women are manipulating them when they do this. The truth of the matter is that for men to remember past experiences the way women do, they *would* have to keep scorecards. Men hang onto the facts but they don't recall, as women do, how an incident made them feel.

The Solution

For Men

Understanding how women view arguments can help men see the wider picture and perhaps avoid making hasty and possibly misguided judgments about a situation.

For Women

Understanding men's view of "arguments" can lead to a powerful insight for women. Men don't like to be part of the problem; they like to be part of the solution. When women expand an argument to talk about patterns they see, men become extremely frustrated. Women feel they are peeling away the layers of an argument to get to the real root of a problem, but men just feel like they are getting further away from a solution. If women are committed to resolving an argument, they should work on helping men understand how apparently unconnected events do bear on the issue at hand and can contribute to finding a solution.

"Success"

What Men Think Success Means

Winning.

What Women Think Success Means

Winning *and* being valued.

The Misunderstanding

Women tell me that the number one reason why they leave their jobs is that they don't feel they're valued for their strengths. Men are perplexed when they hear women say this. What does being valued have to do with success, they wonder? For men, getting a bonus, a pay increase, or a promotion is enough to make them feel valued. Winning and being valued are the same thing. Succeeding according to the male version of success isn't enough for women.

It's easy for men to miss out on this one. "If I don't say anything about her work, it means she's doing a good job. If she's doing a good job, she's valued," they say. But women don't feel like they're at work *just* to produce results. Results alone aren't enough to give them satisfaction. Women often want their work to matter, and to feel this way, they have to hear it from someone.

The Solution

For Men

Understanding women's view of success can provide powerful insights for men. It doesn't take much effort for men to make women feel valued. All they have to do is open their mouths and say what they think instead of taking it for granted that women get it. Women need to *hear* they are appreciated. And it's not because they are insecure. It's because for them, success includes being valued by your colleagues.

For Women

Women need to realize that men don't understand how important being valued is to them. Make some allowances—ask for feedback. Men really may think your bonus or your promotion was enough to make you feel valued.

"How to Listen Effectively"

What Men Do

For men, listening effectively means quietly paying attention and staying focused.

What Women Do

For women, listening effectively means actively participating, nodding or occasionally interjecting to demonstrate that you are attentively following the conversation.

The Misunderstanding

Men often think women are agreeing when women are just showing that they're listening. My husband, a lawyer, tells me he used to fall into this trap during jury trials. While making his final address to the jury, he sometimes noticed that some of the women were nodding. He assumed he had them on his side. But during the opposing lawyer's summation, the same women kept nodding. "It seemed to me the same women were agreeing with opposite positions. I had no idea it was just their way of showing they were listening."

Men demonstrate their attentiveness by sitting still and watching. Even after seeing hundreds of groups of men in my workshops sit and stare at me while I speak, I still get the impression they're not listening, but they are. When women see men sitting stiff and staring while women talk, they may conclude men aren't listening or aren't interested.

Men consider it businesslike to give full attention to what they're hearing. When men watch women actively listening, they can't tell if the women are simply listening or are agreeing with what they hear. When women turn out not to be agreeing at all, it can leave men confused, frustrated, even feeling they are being manipulated. "You can never tell what women mean," they say.

The Solution

For Men

When listening to a woman speaker, it's useful to offer the occasional nod or vocal feedback. "I see what you're saying" will do. It doesn't mean you agree or disagree. It just reassures the speaker that you're following her.

For Women

When women don't see any signs that men are actively listening, they often conclude men aren't paying attention at all. Some women managers have told me that after a presentation, they make men repeat what they said. Needless to say, this kind of patronizing behavior probably doesn't help. Women should not assume that men aren't listening if they are sitting still. The best approach is to check. I often ask men if they agree, or if they understand.

"The Best Way to Convince Is..."

What Men Hear

For men, this means supporting your argument by facts, figures, and careful logic.

What Women Hear

For women, it means supporting your argument by personal experience and the experience of others.

The Misunderstanding

Several years ago, I was in an audience listening to gender anthropologist Dr. Helen Fisher talking about the results of some recent research on how men and women communicate. To illustrate one point, she brought up the experience of some of her own friends. "Just last night I heard some friends say," she began—and a group of men beside me reacted almost immediately. "What does what her friends say have to do with any of this?" they muttered, shaking their heads.

Men think arguments should be supported by facts, figures, and careful logic. Women agree, but they frequently look to personal experience as well. For women, it's a way of being thorough. Women wonder how a solution to a problem might have repercussions in another area. They will weigh a particular decision or strategy against their own experiences or others' experiences as a means of exploring ways it might affect people when it's put into practice. When women bring personal experience into it, men think that's irrelevant. Men look for the facts. They react to women by saying, "What's your personal experience got to do with this?" When men say this, women feel they are dismissing them and disregarding their strengths.

The Solution

For Men

Personal experience can be a valuable resource for understanding problems and coming up with solutions. I know many male business leaders who have come to realize this and now actively seek out the input of their female colleagues, just to get their view.

For Women

Logic, facts, and analysis are important too, particularly if you're trying to convince a man. Try to combine the two approaches to make a case. Ask the men around you for some input and ideas!

Take Responsibility

Where do you start when you want to avoid misunderstandings caused by language? By taking as much responsibility as you can when you listen. If you recognize that gender differences create misunderstanding, it's up to you to do something about it. The key is learning to listen actively.

When we talk, we want to be understood, but that tends to affect how we listen. While the other person is still finishing his or her sentence, we are already formulating a reply. We are busier thinking about what we have to say than making sure we understand what the other person is saying.

My advice? Listen actively. Change gears. Check to make sure you've understood the person you're listening to and make sure you're not listening through the filter of your own assumptions.

You don't need to memorize the misinterpretations I included in the quiz in this chapter. They are just examples of typical words men and women misunderstand when they listen to others "reactively" instead of "actively." Let this chapter plant a seed in your mind to remind you that when you're listening, you might not be hearing what you think you're hearing.

The next chapter will plant another seed in your mind. This seed is about perceptions. Perceptions are our own reality—but not everyone else's—and nowhere is the perceptual gap greater than between women and men. We go through life acting as if the other gender sees what we see. We rarely stop to wonder whether that's true. The unfortunate result, once again, is systematic misunderstandings between men and women. Yet once again, those misunderstandings can be overcome with some quite simple techniques.

7

Perception as Filter: Why Men and Women Live in Different Realities

Understanding means there's nothing to forgive.

—Mother Teresa

If you ask a man and a woman sitting in a room together if they are sitting in the same room, they will almost surely think you're crazy. "Of course it's the same room," they will answer. They're wrong; it is not the same room. Even when they're looking at exactly the same thing, men and women tend to perceive two different realities. The problem is that they end up arguing over which reality actually exists!

Everyone knows what perceptions are. It's "what we take in." What people forget is that our perceptions are just that—impressions taken in through the senses. They are not reality. How we see things depends on what we learned as children, what we absorb from our environment, and, as we saw in Chapter 3, how we're hardwired. I think of perceptions as filters because they shape and even block out other realities. Of course, men and women tend to filter reality in different ways. So it's almost as if we live in entirely different realities. And like the couple in the room, we end up arguing over whose perception is the real one.

A story from a real couple, Matt and Jessica, shows how this happens. When Matt talks about their courting days, he recalls all the problems he encountered trying to get to his first meeting with Jessica's parents. "I was late, and then the car broke down," he says. "But I got there. And I won her!" Matt remembers their courting as a series of snapshot episodes that happened while he was trying to achieve his goal: winning Jessica's hand in marriage. That's Matt's filter.

Jessica doesn't talk about any of the details of Matt's journey to her parents' house. When she thinks of the couple's courting days, she remembers what happened when Matt arrived at the house. She remembers who sat where at the dinner table, how her parents reacted, and the look on Matt's face when he got there. "I remember that your shirt was dirty. And you ate like a pig. It was amazing that my parents didn't try to dissuade me from marrying you!" she says. That's Jessica's perceptual filter.

Matt doesn't remember any of these things. But Jessica sees them as the most important details of the evening. She has no idea why Matt even remembers what happened to him on his way to meet her parents. For her, that's beside the point.

There's nothing surprising about the fact that Matt and Jessica have different versions of their courtship story. Men typically remember events in a very factual manner. For example, Matt remembers the exact time he left to go to Jessica's parents' house and how long it took to get there. Men also tend to think in terms of achieving specific goals. All of Matt's attention was focused on what he had to do in order to get to his destination and win Jessica's hand. It was a challenge to get there and the car broke down. That's what he remembers.

Women, on the other hand, remember things in an interconnected way. They tend to focus on relational aspects of situations. Jessica remembers how the whole process of Matt and her parents getting to know each other unfolded, and she recalls the finer details of everyone's interactions with one another. She recalls the expression on her parents' faces when they saw Matt.

Matt and Jessica joke about how they have such different recollections of the same event. They know they each have a different story, but they don't know why. Even after a quarter century of marriage, neither understands how differently the other looks at life. Instead, Jessica thinks Matt doesn't pay attention to things. "Why do you remember that the car broke down at 6:10 p.m. but you don't remember what you felt like when you met my parents?" she asks him. Matt is mystified as to why Jessica remembers the things she does, like small things her mother said during the meal. "What was so important about that?" he asks her. He thinks she's keeping some kind of scorecard.

Matt and Jessica aren't alone. Men and women are equally mysti-fied by how the other gender sees things. Unless you stop to consider that how the other gender's different filters shape what they perceive, there's a good chance you will miss some essential information.

Men's and Women's Sore Toes   Perpetual filters = auto behavior

We all have perceptual filters. We get them from our upbringing, our environment, our education, and just plain old experience. Usu-ally we don't even know we have them. But they come into play in all facets of our lives, shaping how we perceive what others say and do.

Perceptual filters aren't necessarily bad. They can be very useful. We all need to draw on past experience to make sense of what we see happening around us. We all need frames of reference. The problem is that filters sometimes prevent us from getting all the information we need. Unless we're aware of our filters, we may jump to conclu-sions about what we've observed and risk making mistakes about other people's meanings and intentions.

Men and women are always surprised when I explain how per-ceptual filters affect their communications. We are so used to seeing things the way each of us does that we forget it's only our own per-ception. We assume others perceive events exactly as we do. When they don't, we react. Typically, women think men deliberately ignore things. And typically, men think women read too much into things. It's a frustrating situation, but like Matt and Jessica, we get used to it over the years and we just put up with it. We go into "tolerance" mode. When events happen, we think we are reacting to the events. But really, what we are reacting to is our perceptual filters. Over our lifetime, accumulated perceptual filters get stronger and stronger, shaping our reactions, which, as you'll see, provoke other reactions.

Why does this keep happening? Men and women both have their own comfort zones. We fall into a certain kind of automatic behavior. Women tend to love dealing with details: taking notes, organizing the agenda, analyzing the spreadsheet. Men tend to propose ideas and expect women to execute them. We don't walk around wondering why we think about things the way we do. If we did we wouldn't get any work done. Instead, we develop coping mechanisms to deal with friction. You say to yourself, "That's just the way he (or she) is." You brush it off and carry on.

But there's a danger to this automatic behavior. As you'll see in a moment, it causes some chronic misunderstandings between men and women. I call this "stepping on the other sex's sore toes."

> Imagine you are walking on a beach. The water is sparkling blue and the sun is setting over the ocean and the trees are swaying in the gentle breeze. The problem is you don't notice any of this because you have a sore toe and you've just made it worse by stubbing it on a rock. It's been sore so long that you forgot what you did to it in the first place. You've lived with it for years, so most of the time you don't notice it. But life being as it is, occasionally you'll stub it, or someone comes along and steps on it, and then you can't think of anything else. It just hurts!

Men and women are constantly stepping on each other's sore toes without realizing it. It's certainly not that they want or intend to, it's just that they're unaware that the sore toe exists.

That men and women keep stepping on each other's sore toes is evident in descriptions of the misunderstandings I have heard about in workshop after workshop year after year. Yet there's a simple way to stop stepping on toes and end the misunderstandings. The secret is learning to "frame" what you say, offering your perspective of the situation and then "checking" what the other gender heard to make sure the real message got across. You can't get rid of perceptual filters, but you can avoid many of the misunderstandings they cause.

Women's Sore Toe—"Protective Behavior"

"When I walk into a meeting or a boardroom, I can feel men's behavior change instantly." It is a complaint that is both universal and persistent. You heard the complaint in Chapter 4 from women talking about the challenges involved in working with men. For women who have experienced the change in behavior hundreds of times over their working lives, it can be corrosive. It confirms what women have come to believe: that men really treat women differently.

One of the forms of this "different" treatment is a kind of paternalism that some women also call "protective behavior." Women in our workshops often say that men withhold criticism or soft-pedal criticism when giving them feedback. Women say men also make decisions for women based on the filter, "I can't put a woman in a high-risk assignment or an assignment that involves a lot of traveling."

Other subtler behaviors from male colleagues also strike women as protective. Male colleagues will use offensive language, then turn to the woman in the group and say, "Sorry." As one woman told me, "It's nice when they recognize that swearing is inappropriate, but singling me out and apologizing to me alone is not the solution."

Men's Filter

Where does men's protective behavior come from? I know from experience that men aren't deliberately over-protecting women. But men have been raised with the idea of taking care of women, and that idea creates a perceptual filter that women need protection. Men do make an effort—even unconsciously—to act in ways they were taught are polite or caring.

They are also acting on an unconscious filter that says, "Women need protection." They usually don't even know it. It's not as if they have thought the situation through and come to the conclusion that women need help. It's more like a subtle orientation they were taught to assume toward women. Most men act with the best of intentions. But for women in the business world, getting protective treatment can be a sore-toe experience.

The Solution for Men

Frame your intentions clearly. The first step toward improving communications with women is being direct with them. And trust me, men, you can be more direct with women than you think. For women, being direct translates as "men do care." They find it refreshing to discover that men are thinking about how their actions come across and are willing to take a risk by revealing their concerns. Tell a woman, "I don't mean you to take this personally!" Then tell her what she needs to know. Of course, when women feel men are acting protectively, they should check men's intentions.

Women's Sore Toe—Feeling "Excluded"

Being excluded from men's clubs is not what disturbs women the most. What frustrates women is the sore toe of casual exclusion that gets stepped on every day at work. This happens when men get together in each other's offices without inviting women, or when men never just drop in to women's offices the way they do into men's offices. Women feel that sore toe when men don't include them in male groups and don't make any effort to get to know them. It makes women think that "men don't support us, don't care about us, and don't value us as colleagues."

Every week for years, Margaret, a stockbroker, had witnessed her colleague John invite two other male colleagues out to play sports— squash, golf, hockey—without ever inviting her. As Margaret put it, "What's depressing is that it gets so predictable."

Men's Filter

What was going on? John wasn't deliberately excluding Margaret. He just acted as if he was excluding her because of a perceptual filter that told him she "couldn't possibly be interested in any of these activities." For men, being with other men is simply a comfort zone. "I didn't ask because I didn't think it would be fun for her." A lot of men tell me they feel this way. What they don't realize is that it's a filter. Women want to feel included. When men act on the filtered assumption that women don't want to be included, they step on women's sore toe.

The Solution for Men

Assume nothing, and if you already have assumptions, check them in the office lobby. No, men shouldn't stop playing golf altogether, but they should learn to use a little more imagination in the types of social activities they plan with colleagues. Open up the channels of communication, find a middle ground. Men and women do have specific preferences when it comes to leisure activities, but there are plenty they share too, like wine tasting, laser tag, or even a fitness workout or yoga class at the health club.

If you are creative, you can come up with plenty of win-win solutions. I have seen many companies change their social activities or add some new ones. And men should take note: lots of women play golf, as well as other sports. So don't shy away from asking!

Women's Sore Toe— "Male-Centered Language"

When women and men hear the title chairman or president, they both tend to assume it's a "he." Yet for the rare woman chairman, it's hard not to take this kind of oversight personally. Male-centered language structures feel humiliating to women.

Sports analogies also hit many women's sore toe. I still don't know what an end-around discussion is. Men routinely talk about a level playing field, batting a thousand, or sacking the quarterback when they are discussing business activities. I don't know what these expressions really mean, nor do lots of other women. What's more, we don't care! Military lingo is also common in the business world. But expressions like the war for talent, deploying the troops, and cutting through the prop wash can be alienating for women.

Men's Filter

Women have to understand that men aren't deliberately trying to shut women out when they use this language. Men just have a filter from the past that says that sport and war are effective ways to make everyone understand a point. Not for women! Once upon a time, when the business world was populated almost exclusively by men, it made sense to use sports and military analogies. But that's not true anymore, and such traditionally male-centered language only feeds women's feeling of being excluded. The bottom line is this: it's no longer an effective way to communicate.

The Solution for Men

It's easy: men, use inclusive language. Instead of "Good evening, ladies and gentlemen," try "Good evening, everyone." Everyone will feel welcome. It's not a question of who's right and who's wrong. Just recognize that when you use male-centered language, you lose half your audience. Do your homework; language continues to evolve, and you need to evolve with it.

Women's Sore Toe—Being Discounted or Discredited

It may be a new millennium, but many people still work from the assumption that women generally have fewer skills and less experience than men do. It's ingrained in the minds of most people, men *and* women. But for the women who are on the receiving end of this behavior, it's another sore-toe experience.

I felt this a lot when I was working in sales. Men would overexplain things to me or paraphrase other men's points so I would be sure to understand. They probably weren't even conscious they were doing it. Yet it was demeaning. Women tell me they frequently feel they're being asked for more data or arguments than are necessary, as if men can take it for granted they don't know what they're talking about. At meetings, male colleagues repeat points to their female colleagues— in front of everyone. They seem to assume the women couldn't possibly have understood.

Men's Filter

Men aren't aware they're making women feel discredited. This lack of awareness is most frequent in fields where women don't have a strong historical presence, like finance, the high-ranking civil service, the armed forces, the police, or work areas that require physical labor. In traditional male domains, men have a filter that women "aren't in the right field." The women who have succeeded in those fields frequently share that filter. One woman I spoke to, a retired government official, admitted that she had refused to employ women for many years. "I didn't think many women could handle the work, and I was afraid that if I had too many women working in my office, people would think my work wasn't that important, that it was women's work," she said. She later realized the mistake she had made.

The Solution for Men

Check your behavior to ascertain whether it stepped on your female colleague's sore toe. If you realize it did, tell her it wasn't your intention, and ask her to help you avoid making her feel discredited in the future. She will be happy that you care enough to try to avoid hurting her feelings.

Women's Sore Toe—Male Bonding

For most men, working with other men is a comfort zone. Women notice this, and it may make them feel as if they're being shut out. "Even if two men don't know each other at all," one woman explained it to me, "they seem to instantly identify with each other. It's weird." Men often discuss sports a great deal in their informal conversation, which as you've seen, makes their female peers feel excluded. When women talk to me about this, they refer to it as "male bonding." It's definitely a sore toe for women.

Men's Filter

Women see male bonding as an act of exclusion. But men don't intend for their behavior to send that message. Men tell us it really boils down to "comfort zones." Given the confusion about the rules, it's difficult for men to have a casual conversation with women at work. It seems to men to be safer and easier to talk to other men, and sports is usually a topic of common interest.

The Solution for Men

Find topics of common interest. Get clear on ground rules on subjects that are inclusive. Find out what your female colleagues are interested in. It doesn't mean that you should avoid talking about your favorite topics altogether. Remember that some women love to talk about sports, and some don't, in the same way that some men have other interests. It just makes sense to find out if a topic is of interest to everyone in the room.

Women's Sore Toe—When Men Are Overly Cautious

When men act too formally toward their female colleagues, it comes across to women as if they are keeping their distance. Men can develop a strong sense of collegiality with other men but remain courteous with women. But if this politeness never gives way to a kind of professional familiarity, women feel slighted. A woman concludes the man is insensitive or distant or "doesn't care about me," and from there it's a short trip to "he doesn't take me seriously." It adds to women's feeling of being excluded or dismissed.

Men's Filter

Men's formal behavior doesn't come from indifference toward women. They mean it as a form of respect and as a way to avoid being misinterpreted by women. Men would much rather err on the side of formality than be blamed for being too familiar with their female colleagues. Men are genuinely afraid of offending women.

The Solution for Men

You probably guessed what I'm going to say. Don't hide behind your comfort zone. Make sure to keep the communication channels open, and you will no longer be concerned about offending because you will know what works.

Women's Perceptual Filters

As noted in Chapter 4, it's hard to get men to talk about the challenges they face when working with women. Typically, men don't spend as much time thinking about relationships with their colleagues as women do. "We go to work to do a job," they say. But this doesn't mean men don't feel challenges working with women. Asking the question the right way is the key to getting men to talk. For instance, they don't think about whether women make them feel disempowered, but they will talk about what makes them pull back.

Women certainly do step on men's sore toes. And they do so because of perceptual filters that make them look at the world in a certain way.

You will now see the behavior that makes men pull back. Women, watch how your behavior sometimes comes across to men. Understanding your own perceptual filters is the first step to avoiding the misunderstandings they lead to.

Men's Sore Toe—"When Women Don't Articulate Problems Clearly"

Men in our workshops routinely complain that "women throw one conversation into another," or that when women discuss a problem, "they drag all sorts of other problems into it." It's true. When women tackle problems, they look for solutions by expanding the problem into other issues. Men find this frustrating. To them, it sounds as though women are just adding new problems to the pot, obscuring the issue at hand and getting further from a solution. "When I present a problem," as one man put it, "women come up with a whole series of other problems. I don't know which problem we're focusing on." Some men conclude from this that women just aren't focused and that they're not very good problem solvers. Others say that women are vague, they're chaotic, they meander.

Women's Filter

Women are not vague or chaotic or less focused than men. They do not meander. They just automatically see issues in terms of how one problem is linked to another. Women use talking to find the focus. Men focus first, then talk. It's not a better or worse way to see problems. It's just different. For a man, the problem is a single one. He wants clarity on it before anything else happens. Women don't stop to think that when men hear the word "problem," they don't really hear the same thing as women.

The Solution for Women

Frame your conversation first. Before you even open your mouth, think about what it is you need from the man with whom you are having this conversation. If you are looking to explore a problem before even trying to solve it, you'll have to say so. Men assume you want a solution—end of story!

Men's Sore Toe—"Women Generalize"

"Women are always taking one situation and expanding it to generalize about a whole lot of things." That's a frequent male complaint in the workshops we hold. But what men call generalizing is really seeing patterns. Women tend to remember the patterns in things and use that information to analyze present circumstances. Men find this frustrating because it comes across to them as blame, or as "dragging things back from the past." They complain that women extrapolate universals from a single specific. As one man put it, "a woman takes one situation and then makes it sound as if I'm always like that." If he shows up late, the woman chides him for being "always late." Perhaps he is often late, but to him it feels like a sophisticated form of blame.

Women's Filter

When women generalize, they aren't setting out to blame. They are just behaving naturally. Women tend to look at events and see patterns. Women remember similar behaviors from past situations and match them up. And when they see a pattern, they do tend to attribute it to someone's character. They can't help it (and sometimes they're right). The problem is that they forget that men don't see the world the way they do. A woman will think she's making an observation, but a man will hear her generalizing, "score-keeping," and blaming him. When women can't name the patterns they see, they will feel frustrated.

The Solution for Women

Drop the words "always" and "never" from your vocabulary. I know it's hard because you can easily see the pattern in situations. But these two words only invite men to argue about the actual frequency of an incident. In your discussions with men, as much as possible, keep things isolated and specific to the point at hand. Men tend not to see patterns; they want to stay focused on one issue, sort it out, and move on.

Men's Sore Toe—"Women Get Emotional"

Men insist that the kinds of things that make women upset "would just bounce off me." No wonder they sometimes "just want to tell women to get over it." In fact, women are not more sensitive than men. They just process information differently. Women tend to internalize things. They often think first of how they may have affected an event or situation. They wonder what they might have done to cause an outcome. They internalize conflict, while men externalize it. Men sometimes interpret women's reaction as demonstrating a lack of confidence or as weakness.

Women's Filter

Internalizing conflict, for women, is like breathing. It just happens. There's no hidden agenda in women's way of reacting to conflict. Once men understand this, it becomes a tremendously useful insight in their dealings with women, and much of the uncertainty and apprehension in dealing with their female colleagues falls away.

The fact that tears in the workplace, for women, are almost always an expression of frustration and anger, just as thumping a desk might be for a man, is a real "Ah-hah" for most men. They can now replace the filter "Women are sensitive" with "Women feel stress and conflict differently and express anxiety differently from men."

The Solution for Men

Relax! Crying does not mean women are falling apart. Most of the time there's nothing for you to do but listen while women express their frustration. Pass the tissue, and let women clear the air and vent their frustrations.

Men's Sore Toe—"Why Don't Women Correct Inappropriate Behavior?"

"I wish women would just tell me what's the matter. Instead, they walk off in a huff, and then bring it up days later!" That's a common lament from men, and it's a fair one, for that's truly how women behave. They often do hesitate before telling men they're unhappy about certain behavior. Why? Most women are afraid that when they confront men about their behavior, they'll be brushed off or dismissed as overly sensitive.

Women's Filter

There are reasons why women don't confront men immediately about inappropriate behavior. Women are acting on the filter "Men dismiss us." Women don't want to appear petty for addressing one incident, so instead they make a mental note and observe and if it happens again, that's when they address it. Or they will wait until a later time to bring it up, when they feel it may be more appropriate or they're on safer ground. They feel if their case is stronger, they are in less danger of getting the brush-off.

The Solution for Women

Telling men straightaway—in private—is the best policy. Keep remembering that, for the most part, men's actions aren't intended as personal slights. It's a challenge to be straightforward about your reactions, but doing so will free you from the burden of constantly mulling things over in your head. If you get stuck, refer to the methods we'll discuss in Chapter 10.

Men's Sore Toe—"Women Don't Get to the Point"

Men complain that women fail to understand their need to get to the bottom line. "Women talk around the point without seeming to move toward a solution," they say. It's an especially sensitive issue in their personal lives. A man will be driving with his wife to a restaurant and she will say, "Remember that great Chinese restaurant we went to last year? It's just around the corner." His reaction? "Yes, I remember." And he keeps driving to the original destination. When his wife is hurt that he didn't get the message, he's perplexed and frustrated and feels like he's being blamed for something without knowing exactly what he did wrong.

Women's Filter

At work, this translates into a classic misunderstanding between men and women. Men say a woman will beat around the bush and then "blame me because I couldn't read her mind." What they don't understand is that women are acting on a filter. What seems to men like an obscure reference shows up to a woman as a "direct hit." Women don't understand why men don't see that a passing remark about the restaurant is really a suggestion to actually go there. Men just think it's a historical observation and don't take it any further.

The Solution for Women

When you communicate to men, be more direct. Don't be pushy, but use clear, action-oriented language. Frame your conversation: "I have a request; I would love you to do this for me." Men will be happy to hear requests this way.

Take Ownership of Your Filters

Do we own our perceptual filters or do they own us? Many people have difficulty imagining that filters are just part of who they are. At the beginning of one of our workshops, we heard very forthrightly from David, a particularly brash manager, who insisted he didn't have any filters at all. "You can't change the way I am," he said. "I'm a control freak and that's that." David certainly acted like a control freak. I remember watching his colleagues shudder as he summarily silenced them mid-sentence. When his colleagues spoke, he would hold up his hand like a football referee and tell them to "hold that thought" (of course, they always forgot it before he gave them a chance to speak). When they tried to explain their points of view, he interrupted them.

The answer to the question is this: filters own us until we become aware of them, recognize them, and take ownership of them.

During the course of the workshop, David was able to recognize that he had a filter, one that said, "You have to act 'controlling' to be in control." That filter came from a specific experience early in his career when his partners abandoned him. "I made a decision at that point that it was better to control everything myself than to be left high and dry, and I've held on to that philosophy ever since."

David recognized his filter. He could see that his behavior didn't really come naturally to him at all and that it was actually counterproductive. Things did get done, but he left a wake of frustrated and discouraged colleagues behind him. More important, he understood that his controlling behavior was actually defeating his real commitment to help his team accomplish its goals.

So he took responsibility for his filter. He decided to change his behavior. It really was that simple. Once he had been able to see his filters, he was able to change his behavior and work toward his real goal.

David's story ended well, but it could easily have led to many challenges at his company. David's perceptual filter had created a blind spot. He simply didn't see how his actions were perceived by his colleagues. In the next chapter, you'll hear how men and women's perceptual filters create typical blind spots, which lead to huge misunderstandings. And you'll see what you can do to avoid being a victim of your blind spots.

8

Assumptions and Blind Spots

Your assumptions are your windows on the world. Scrub them off every once in a while, or the light won't come in.

—Alan Alda

Stereotypes - oversimplified sheer myth.

In the water most of us swim in at work, stereotypes are routinely assumed and accepted: "Men don't listen," "Women talk too much," "Women prefer administrative work—and they're so good at it," "For women, career isn't their first priority," "Men are the primary income earners." You've probably heard a few more. These stereotypes—any stereotypes—can be blatant or subtle. By definition, they are at best oversimplified, at worst sheer myths. Yet the real problem is not really the ideas themselves. The real problem is what we do with them. As with all myths, once these stereotypes plant themselves in our consciousnesses, we act on them without checking to see if they are true. Often, they are not. *assumptions= blind spots, major cause of misunderstanding*

The result is blind spots, things we don't see because the stereotypes have obstructed our vision. Assumptions we've made about how the other gender will react or what they will think in certain situations prevent us from getting the real information from the person. Such blind spots are a major cause of misunderstanding between the sexes.

Maya's Story

As Maya's story shows, blind spots can be dangerous for both the individuals involved and the company. In this case, which is typical, a blind spot almost ruined a working relationship and very nearly pushed a valuable employee out of a company. You may recognize yourself in one of the central characters.

Maya, an engineer, mother of three, and one of the top technical experts in a large computer firm, had decided to leave her job. When I met her, she was already considering an offer from a rival firm. It was a familiar story. After years of working hard with stunning results, she felt her bosses still didn't appreciate her work. She decided enough was enough.

Maya enjoyed her job and got along well with her colleagues, so I probed her to find out in more detail why she had decided to leave. It turned out her company had decided to open a new division in Australia. Although it would not mean a promotion, Maya had felt she was the ideal candidate for the position of project manager in this large, high-profile venture, which would require a three-month stay abroad. But the job had not been offered to her; in fact, she only heard about it after learning that someone else, less qualified than she, was being considered for the position. No one had asked *her* if she was interested. Maya was so humiliated and offended by this that she decided to not even bring it up with her boss. As far as she was concerned, it was proof he didn't respect her or recognize her qualifications. "It's clear what he thinks of me. It's because I'm a woman."

I suspected a blind spot in Maya and asked her if she was willing to test her assumptions by asking her boss why he hadn't considered her for the Australia job. It was not an easy step for her, since she had already made up her mind to leave, but she decided to give it a go. "Leave your assumptions at the door. They may be right, but forget them for a minute," I told her. Instead of telling him she was hurt, which would put him on the defensive, I told her to "frame" her comments. So this is what she said:

"Mark, I have assumed that you didn't even consider me for the position in Australia. I want to check that assumption."

Mark was floored. "I just assumed that a woman like you with three small children wouldn't want to pack up in the middle of the school year and move to Australia for three months," he said. "I didn't want to put you on the spot and make you decline."

Mark was in many ways a typical sales manager. He was an "action" man—committed, aggressive, and results-oriented. He was used to living by the rules of a reactive environment where there wasn't much time to sit back and reflect on things. But he was also a fair man who tried to look out for his colleagues' best interests. He knew Maya was perfect for the job, and he had agonized over whether to ask her or not. But in the end, he had thought it would hurt her to offer her the job.

Maya was stunned and angry, but she could see that Mark meant well. Most importantly, she could see that the situation was salvageable. "This job in Australia would be the best thing that could happen to me," she told him. "I have been waiting for an opportunity like this to come up for years!"

Where Was the Blind Spot?

Maya and Mark both had blind spots—preconceptions about what the other thought based on stereotypical ideas they had about the opposite gender. Mark had assumed Maya put family first. He had decided not to offer the job to Maya because he had thought that she wouldn't want to disrupt her family life with a move to Australia. Maya had assumed that Mark didn't respect women. Because of that assumption, she concluded that she had been unfairly and unreasonably discriminated against because of her gender.

Luckily, they recognized their blind spots before it was too late. Mark offered Maya the job in Australia. Maya got special permission for her children to miss some school and they and her husband flew over to join her for a month. When she got back, she said it had been one of the most challenging and exciting projects she had ever worked on.

Blind Spots at Home

Blind spots can be costly for everyone, and not just at work. Several years ago a young executive named Victoria came to me for advice about a marriage breakdown. Victoria had been on a retreat to "think and refocus herself." On returning, she had decided to get a divorce. She said to me, "The relationship has changed. All Tim wants to do is spend time apart, each of us doing our own thing."

Victoria assumed Tim was losing his commitment to the marriage and losing interest in her. Like many people, she sought relief from questioning her relationship by actively seeking a resolution. She went off on a retreat and came back with a decision. She made an assumption about the meaning of Tim's actions, sealed that box shut, and moved on to action—which in this case, meant getting a divorce.

It turned out that Victoria had a blind spot. Like Maya, she had assumed men don't care. I encouraged her to tell Tim about her assumptions before she announced that she wanted a divorce. When she did, Tim couldn't believe his ears. He said he was as committed to the marriage as ever. And there was a good explanation for his actions. Tim felt strongly that couples needed to be independent.

As his relationship with Victoria grew, he worried they were getting "too fused." He reacted by scheduling more outings with his friends and by encouraging her to do more with her friends too. He just assumed Victoria thought as he did and would automatically understand. Luckily, Victoria and Tim realized they had made wrong assumptions about each other before it was too late.

Blind Spots Are Self-Perpetuating

Men and women everywhere tend to make the same assumptions about each other and often end up with the same blind spots. Then they take the same actions based on those blind spots. The real tragedy is that those actions usually end up feeding the original assumptions.

Take women's assumption that men don't listen. Women often react to this assumption by actually talking more. Women tell me, "Since men don't listen, I feel I have to talk more, explain more, and repeat myself a lot. If I talk long enough he'll eventually catch on." How do men react when women keep talking to them? They stop listening, because they know it's been said before and will be said again. Then what happens? Women think they have the proof of their original assumption that men don't listen.

Breaking the Cycle

How do we avoid becoming victims of self-perpetuating blind spots? The first thing to do is to question assumptions we are making. It's hard, but there is no way around it.

The clue is learning to listen. There are two ways of listening. Most of us just use listening as a screening process. We wait to hear what we already know, then decide if it's "right" or "wrong." When you listen this way, all you are doing is validating your own opinions and assumptions. You're not really learning anything new.

What you need to do is listen actively. Active listening means consciously interrupting your screening process so that you can really learn new things or new ways of looking at the old things. You have to turn listening into an opportunity to learn, put aside your assumptions and opinions, and become open to new discoveries, some of which might well challenge the very assumptions and opinions you previously held. Active listening lets you stand in the other person's shoes as you learn from, and about, their perspective. It lets you get inside the other person's head to see what they're really saying. Active listening is what gives you those "Ah-hah" moments.

How do you do that?

Follow these guidelines:

1. **Check your assumptions at the door.** Recognize that perceptions, which may be incorrect, tend to stand in for reality.

2. **Take ownership of the situation.** It's the only way to avoid becoming a victim of your own blind spots. Try to recognize your blind spots before you judge and evaluate others. Ask yourself, "Is there something in what this person is saying that I'm not understanding?" There probably is.

3. **Ask questions.** Ask the person you're listening to what they mean. What's their opinion on the issue? How does this appear to them?

4. **Use checking and framing strategies.** Recognize that there could be more to a situation than you think. Then frame your

question in a way that avoids putting your boss or employee or colleague—or spouse—on the defensive.

5. **Don't rationalize or screen the responses you get.** Ask yourself whether you are having a true dialogue with the other person. If you're in a true dialogue, if you're really listening actively, it means you're learning something about the other person's perspective that you never thought of before. You're trying to stand in the other person's shoes and see the world from their vantage point.

6. **Don't get on the defensive yourself.** "What you said hurt me" is not a good way to get honest feedback. Take ownership of your assumptions. Confess and confirm: "I made an assumption about what you said to me. I just want to check and see if that's what you really meant."

7. If you need to remind yourself about why it's so important to at least question and probably put away your assumptions, **ask yourself some simple questions:** What is my long-term commitment here? Do I want to make this relationship work?

Over the years I have noticed there are some assumptions men repeatedly make about women and some assumptions women repeatedly make about men. All the assumptions create blind spots that lead to misunderstandings. The solutions are usually simpler than you think. Have a look at the following:

Men's Blind Spots

Here are some of the assumptions men make about women.

"You have to be careful with women."

What Men Assume

Men often assume they have to watch their step with women, their assumption being that women are more sensitive. The assumption usually comes from experience. Men may have seen women get emotional over difficult situations at work and want to avoid provoking women at all costs. Many men come to me asking for advice on how to talk to female employees. They know they have a communication problem. They are holding back, watching what they say, and they can tell it doesn't work, but they don't know what to do. When men rank the things that make them most uncomfortable in dealing with women at work, the highest score for the most discomfiting task goes to giving critical feedback to women; it makes men very, very uncomfortable.

Ernesto, a senior bank manager, was one of those men. "I'm harder on the men who work for me than I am on the women," Ernesto admits. "I march forward with the men, but I'm always soft-pedaling with the women. I mean, sometimes I really dress the men down. I'll even tease them, say, about their tie or something. But I won't so much as comment on what women are wearing!" To his credit, Ernesto had already put two and two together. "Women tell me they think I'm not listening. And the truth is, I pull back with women. I definitely treat the men and women in my company differently. I have to! Women take things so personally!"

Like many men, Ernesto assumed that women take things personally. I urged him to check that assumption.

Finding the Blind Spot

The truth is, women often do take things personally. As we saw in Chapter 3, because of the way women's brains work, they don't separate emotions from the rest of their brain processes in the same way that men do. But the fact that women react emotionally to situations doesn't mean they "can't take it."

That's what Ernesto found out when he scheduled a meeting with the women on his executive committee to check his assumption. He told his female colleagues: "I have had an insight recently that I make an assumption that women always take things personally. I realize that I soft-pedal with women to avoid that. Do you feel that I do this, and if so, how can I address issues differently with you?"

The women's reaction? "It's true!" they all said. "We do take things personally." Then they delivered the really surprising news. "What's the problem?" they asked Ernesto. "As long as we know you're being straightforward with us, that's what really matters. What really hurts is when you beat around the bush with us."

What Ernesto discovered, by checking with his female employees, was that he had a blind spot. With the best of intentions, he had assumed that the women wanted to be treated with particular tact and delicacy, that direct feedback would hurt their feelings, and that he had better step lightly. He was completely wrong. What the women wanted was to be treated in the same way as the men.

"Women are more comfortable dealing with women."

So it's okay to let women?

What Men Assume

It happens all the time. A woman walks into the car showroom, and the male sales reps automatically withdraw and let the lone female step forward for the attempt at a sale. The widow of the recently deceased investment client is quickly reassigned to the sole female investment advisor. Men just assume that women are better equipped to deal with other women's problems and that women clients or colleagues are more comfortable dealing with other women. They probably get this idea from their upbringing and socialization. Women may even unwittingly reinforce this idea when they create "women's" committees for various activities. Wherever this assumption comes from, men act on it without checking it, and they simply shift responsibility for dealing with women onto other women. Men ask women to get into groups to work on women's issues in a company, or they send a woman to take care of a personal problem with another woman in their company. In sales or services, it is just assumed that women prefer dealing with members of their own gender. It's an assumption that most companies act on without testing.

A large retail store that sells men's clothing called me to deal with the following problem. Years earlier, the store had reacted to a study that found out most men's clothes were actually bought by women. "All our salesmen are men," they said, "so we employed some women in sales." The problem? It backfired. The saleswomen actually had a *harder* time selling to women. They even had the feeling that the women who came into the store were avoiding them.

I told the store's management that it might have a blind spot. I suggested it conduct some focus groups with women, carefully framing their questions. Managers at the store assembled the focus groups and asked them: "We have been making the assumption that women don't like to buy from men. Is it true?"

Finding the Blind Spot

Well, the assumption was partially true. The women said they didn't like buying from men. But the company had a blind spot. Women said they were uncomfortable buying men's clothes simply because the salesmen didn't know how to treat them. They repeatedly said that they didn't necessarily want to be served by women. "We just want to be taken seriously by male salespeople," they said. Women said that if the men knew how to treat them, they preferred salesmen to saleswomen, since they wanted a man's input on their purchases. "Train your salesmen on how to treat women shoppers," the women said.

Many companies resist seeing this kind of blind spot. Why? Companies often make large investments based on wrong assumptions, so they aren't too open to seeing their blind spots. This company had employed female sales staff thinking it would solve the problem; they weren't eager now to start again with a different solution.

Do women really prefer dealing with women and women's issues? No. Professional women don't want to be stuck in women's ghettos, no matter what kind of company they work for.

"Women can't handle tough work or tough clients."

"Toughness" is a mutable concept, as I saw for myself one day in New York when I went into the local wine store to buy a bottle of Champagne for a celebration at the office. I suddenly heard loud singing—the song was "Roxanne"—and turned to see a guy wearing a headset, dancing in time to the song, utterly oblivious to the other shoppers, and clearly very high on some form of controlled substance. The two security officers in the store, one male, one female, noticed him at once. "Let's take him out!" said the male officer, his hand forming a fist. "Hold it a minute," said the female officer, restraining her colleague with a gentle touch.

She went over to the disruptive customer, started singing along with him, and then more or less took him in her arms and danced him out of the store.

The remaining customers applauded. The security officer's actions had defused their fear and left them smiling. No one, including the very inebriated singer, was hurt, and the entire "incident" ended much better than if the male officer had exhibited the clichéd "toughness" he was so ready to put into action.

So what's the tougher challenge: lashing out or defusing a potentially volatile, potentially dangerous moment? Police departments prefer the latter—theoretically, anyway—and studies by police departments like New York's confirm that the presence of women is more likely to defuse a situation than a display of male "toughness" will. It's something for businesses to think about as well.

What Men Assume

Men tend to make two assumptions about tough clients: that those clients will prefer dealing with men, and that women won't want to deal with them anyway. Almost certainly, this is another assumption that derives from men's socialization. The attitude is particularly prevalent for women in fields not traditionally welcoming to women, like the police. I saw it in action in a workshop with the Los Angeles Police Department, where women were systematically relegated to lower-risk positions like traffic and clerical work.

The "tough client" scenario is even more prevalent. Salim, a manager at an international consulting firm, told me he avoided sending women out to work with some of his clients. "I've got this male client from the Middle East," he told me. "I could never send a woman to work with him, for his sake and for hers. He would resist working with a woman and she would pay the price for it. In his eyes, a woman can be an administrative assistant—nothing more." Salim repeated that he wasn't passing any kind of judgment either on his client or on his female colleagues. It was just a situation he assumed it was best to avoid, he said, for practical reasons. The problem was that he had a female colleague, Mary, who was perfectly qualified and well suited to work for this particular client; she had been a member of a team that worked on an earlier project for him.

Finding the Blind Spot

Salim had two blind spots, one with his client and one with Mary. I pointed out that he was acting on two assumptions and I pushed him to test them. "Could you be making assumptions about your client and Mary that could both be wrong?" I asked. Salim said he was positive the client didn't respect women. So I asked him, "What makes you so sure he'll react to Mary with the kind of resistance you assume he would exhibit?"

Salim said he was willing to test his assumptions. He checked with Mary. "I'm assuming you wouldn't want to work with this client. Am I right?" he asked.

Mary's answer surprised him. "I'd love to work for this client," she said. "I know his file and I know his business inside out. I know what he needs. It would be a great challenge." And she added, "I also know from experience that he doesn't treat all women as administrative assistants, there to do his bidding."

Then Salim decided to test the assumptions he had made about the client's preference for men. He told the client, "I think I've got the best person for the position of team leader on your project. I've hesitated because the candidate is a woman, and I know the project will involve you being together a lot. I have assumed you wouldn't be comfortable with that." And then Salim told him it was Mary.

The client's answer? "Oh, Mary," he said. "I remember her. I'd love to meet her again." The client revealed that he thought she had done outstanding work in the past, from what he had seen, and he loved her style. So Salim decided to give Mary the job, after all.

Assuming women don't want to take risks creates a big blind spot for men. Women love challenges as much as men do. Those who are courageous enough to enter nontraditional fields are certainly risk takers to begin with. They can deal with tough clients when it's necessary, just as men can—and they can often "read" clients in ways that allow them to find other ways around problems.

Women's Blind Spots

Men aren't the only ones who make stereotypical judgments about the opposite gender. Women's assumptions about men also create blind spots.

"Men like the status quo."

What Women Assume

Lots of women—particularly those in the denial stage of gender awareness—think men don't want anything to change. They believe men are more than happy with the "traditional business model" and the traditional work environment. Or they believe that deep down, most men would rather go back to the "good old days" before they had to work with women.

Christina, a human resources manager at a pharmaceutical firm, made this assumption. She had been trying to address gender issues at work for years, but said she couldn't even get the conversation started. Her explanation? "Men just want to keep things the way they are. As far as I'm concerned, if I want things to change, I'll have to leave and try somewhere else."

Christina felt that she knew this for a fact, but in reality, she had made some assumptions based on what she had observed. There had been several cases of harassment at her bank and she had the mandate to address the issue with 15 senior executives, all men. Whenever she tried to get things like harassment or equal opportunities on the agenda at meetings, she felt resistance from them. "Men don't bring gender issues up on their own," she explained. "It's never on the agenda." She had overheard some male colleagues joke about "the good old days." They'd heard from the older generation about a time, the "good old days," before there was "harassment training" and the push to recruit more women. "I give up!" she told me.

Finding the Blind Spot

Christina had a blind spot. There may be one in a thousand men in the working world these days who wishes for the return of the good old days. Every human resources survey shows this: men want change too, especially—but not only—younger men. Studies have shown that a decisive majority of men would choose quality of life over more money or promotion, if they had the choice.

So I challenged Christina to test her assumption. "Is it possible you are making assumptions about your colleagues based on your own filter that men don't care?" I asked. It took her a year to decide to check her assumptions, but she eventually did and then she saw her blind spot. "I have the assumption that you don't want anything to change," she announced at a meeting with the 15 executives. "All we talk about is keeping shareholders happy, net profits, and growth. We never talk about the workplace environment. Is it true that no one here cares about our workplace environment?"

The answer was a resounding "No." Fourteen of the 15 executives said they really wanted change. They thought the environment at the firm was difficult and there were too many "power plays," too much condescending behavior, and too many put-downs between colleagues.

"So," Christina asked, "why have we never talked about these things at meetings?" Their answer really took her unawares. "It was never on the agenda," they said. At meetings, the executives felt pushed to address exactly what was on the agenda and get through it. They were aware there were problems in the workplace environment. Many had read about harassment and had thought about it. Many expressed the desire for a more inclusive and diverse work environment. Several feared the company was getting a reputation for having a harassing environment and wanted to do something about it, but they didn't know what to do. Their tendency to be goal-oriented and focus on business priorities made them stick to the agenda in meetings.

Christina had a blind spot. She thought men didn't care when actually, men were just acting in a normal, natural male work style: they followed the agenda in a logical way. When she put "workplace environment" on the agenda, the executives were happy to collaborate on research and to address problems in the working environment.

"Men are insensitive."

What Women Assume

Women constantly see situations at work in which men don't react the way the women think they should. Someone will criticize a woman at a meeting and she will tell a coworker afterward, "He should have stood up for me." What do women conclude when men act this way? That men are insensitive. Women complain that men don't notice women's reactions. After experiencing a difficult situation at work, women say the men around them just carry on as if nothing happened.

Finding the Blind Spot

The head of a section in the U.S. Department of Justice (DOJ) sent a group of ten top prosecutors—four women and six men—to one of our gender intelligence workshops in an attempt to stimulate more cooperation and higher productivity in the group. The day started with the women at one table and the men at another, like distant islands.

The women wasted no time complaining about the men's insensitivity. They brought up a recent case of assault during which the men had been focused solely on getting a guilty verdict and showed no interest in the healing that the victim and his family were trying to effect. For the women, spending time with the family was one aspect of the justice they had sworn to achieve; for the men, a guilty verdict that would vindicate the victim was the key to the family's healing.

This was textbook gender-difference science, just as we saw it in Chapter 3: the men were transactional and converging on the single goal; the women were widening the context to insist that winning included transformation.

In fact, it was the science taught in the workshop that made both men and women realize there was nothing to forgive; this was the way the two genders operated. For the women, it taught them that the men were not insensitive; rather, they turned their emotions toward the object of winning the case—period. For the men, the lesson was that the healing the women pursued was in no way "beside the point." For the DOJ, the workshop was a lesson in the worth of matching a male and female prosecutor so that both aspects of justice could be realized.

The truth is that most men are more sensitive than they appear to be to the women they work with. It's a big blind spot for women who interpret men's "detachment" as lack of feeling or insensitivity. The male prosecutors put their emotions aside in order to achieve their goal, leaving the women prosecutors to assume they didn't have any feelings at all. The trap they fell into was in assuming that the men were cold and heartless, when really they just showed a classic male tendency—emotional containment. You respect the case you're trying by not laying bare your own feelings.

What's going on? Men have emotions, but they deal with them differently from the way women do. Even as little boys, men are taught to suppress their emotions by not showing them. Later, in the traditional work environment, they are taught to depersonalize things and to deal with problems in a detached, rational way. In other words, all their lives men are told to take charge of their emotions. So that's what they do. Women need to understand men's way of dealing with emotions before they jump to conclusions about men not caring.

"Men think they own the leadership role."

What Women Assume

Women who work in teams or in partnerships with men often live through this scenario: when the list of tasks for a project is being created, the man will automatically take the high-profile tasks. "I'll do that one," he'll say. From the women's point of view, the man wants to be in the limelight while they're stuck in the background doing research and taking notes! When men act this way, women assume it means men think they can do things better themselves.

Leslie and Alan, sales partners in a software company, were in this typical situation. According to Leslie, every time they had their weekly sales meeting to decide on goals and tasks, she would listen, assessing what she could do best before she took on any tasks. While she was thinking, however, Alan stepped up and grabbed all the tasks he wanted. He ended up giving the presentations to clients, making the business case, and brainstorming with clients about new product markets. Leslie was left doing all the background work and research for Alan. She saw Alan's behavior as a direct message to her, and she assumed he simply didn't think she was capable of handling the higher profile tasks. She even suspected Alan was *afraid* of letting her take this work on because he didn't want to have to pick up the pieces if she failed! "Alan thinks I can't do anything, so he won't even let me take risks," she said.

Finding the Blind Spot

I pressed Leslie to check her own perceptions to see if she had a blind spot. At their next sales meeting, she brought up the subject head-on. "I assume you think I can't do higher profile tasks directly with the client," she said to Alan. He was stunned. He had never doubted that she could do these things; it had just never occurred to him that he was grabbing the riskier, high-profile work for himself and shutting her out.

How could Alan not see what he was doing? The answer is that he was acting on instinct. As we have seen, men's working style is action-oriented and results-driven. Whereas women get their sense of fulfillment from things like building relationships, men's sense of achievement comes from getting results. That's what makes men feel that they're making their best contribution. And it's a huge blind spot for women, who think there's more behind men's actions than men are telling them.

In private, men reveal their true feelings about women's capabilities. The truth is that many men suspect their women colleagues do the job better than they can. Men say, "Women are more detail-oriented and more organized. They do their homework and come to meetings better prepared."

Women have a huge blind spot when they assume men think they are incapable. When men act according to their action-oriented working style, they are not trying to imply that women are incompetent. They are just doing what comes naturally to them. Women have to understand men's style and not let it get to them. Here's a case in point:

Diana had worked hard on the presentation to be delivered in Geneva to an international gathering of client CEOs. This mother of two young children had stayed late at the office and given up two weekends with her family to devote her considerable intelligence and energies to the case she had outlined to Brian, her highly approving, seemingly supportive boss. After the long overnight flight from Chicago, Diana met Brian, as planned, outside the conference room and was stunned as he took the deck of slides out of her hands and said, "I've got it now." As she later told me, Brian then "waltzed into the room and did an inadequate and incompetent job of delivering the presentation."

She had been, she told me, "stupefied" by his action—by the way he took command of her work. She was also hurt by it. But women cannot let stupefaction and hurt feelings detour them from getting their due. There was a simple response Diana could have given when Brian grabbed the deck from her. "No," she should have said, taking the deck right back from him, "*I've* got it. This is my work. I know it thoroughly, and I can deliver it more effectively than you can." That might have left Brian standing there stupefied, but it would have been Diana who gave the presentation.

Women must stand up for themselves and grab some of the work they want instead of waiting for it to be offered to them. It's time to break through the assumption that men own the leadership role. How do you break through? With this, as with all assumptions, the key is active listening. Active listening means you "check" your assumptions before you jump to conclusions about the behavior of the other gender. Always make sure you understand the real reasons the other gender is acting a certain way before you take any actions. As you have seen, there's a good chance you have a blind spot. Letting it control you can lead to difficult misunderstandings.

[handwritten note: ← Women blindspot - assuming men think women aren't capable]

9

Understanding Our Strengths

Gettin' good players is easy. Gettin' 'em to play together is the hard part.

—Casey Stengel, baseball manager

Although we're all born knowing that men and women are different, the previous chapters have shown us just how different we really are. We look around us at the same world, but men see it one way and women another. We hear different things when we listen to the same words. And we don't speak the same language.

You've seen the challenges that arise when you don't understand how different the other gender is, and you've seen what you can do to overcome those challenges and improve your working relationship with the opposite gender.

What you might not know is how advantageous for all businesses everywhere the differences between men and women can be. They are actually a huge source of strength—once we understand the differences.

Remember Sandra, the lawyer, and Nathan, the manager of The Body Shop? We met them both at the beginning of this book, in work situations in which both felt that their skills and qualities were not being recognized or well used. And that was true; both possessed special skills their colleagues didn't recognize. If the colleagues had only known how to make use of these special skills, they would have seen how valuable Sandra and Nathan were.

Sandra could build strong relationships with her clients. She could see problems from angles few of her male colleagues would have imagined. Nathan was skilled at sticking to an agenda, steering meetings to a conclusion, and initiating action. He was able to get to the root of things when his colleagues sometimes got bogged down in the details of a problem.

The big challenge in today's working world is to create an environment where both men and women flourish. The way to do that is simple. Learn what men's and women's special strengths are, and work out how to put them to use.

Men and women have different approaches to almost all day-to-day activities at work. Both can be valuable. Sometimes the women's approaches will get better results. Sometimes the men's approaches will. The key is flexibility. You have to understand what the differences are and how each approach can work to advantage in a given situation.

Here are ten areas where men's and women's approaches and working styles differ. Learn to spot these differences and use them to your advantage. You'll be amazed at the results.

Management Styles

Women typically have a consensus-driven style that focuses on creating relationships as much as on achieving specific objectives. Women tend to be inclusive in their approach to managing. They stay the course until they achieve consensus, making sure they get everyone's opinion before they make a decision. Women also tend to direct others by making suggestions.

Men managers usually see their job as getting everyone else onboard. They often make a decision before consulting others. Then they try to convince others to subscribe to their vision. Men's style is typically oriented toward meeting an objective. "Let's just get it done," men say. Men tend to direct by telling others what to do as opposed to suggesting a course of action.

The Benefits of Both Approaches

Women's collaborative approach to managing is extremely effective for brainstorming, for coming up with creative new ideas. Yet men's style is probably more effective in emergency situations, when a decision absolutely must be made and carried out quickly. The point is not that only women should brainstorm and only men should get things done. Each gender should learn to look to the other for input when faced with different business challenges.

Problem Solving

When women take on problem solving, they generally try to make sure all aspects of the problem have been well covered before they take action. Their approach is intuitive and contextual. As you have seen, women tend to get to the bottom of things by talking them through. They cast a wide net of ideas before arriving at a conclusion. Women also try to build consensus to solve problems, even as they explore how possible solutions may affect other people or other areas of a business. Women, therefore

✓ Collaborate.

✓ Focus on the long term.

✓ Take lots of factors into consideration.

✓ Can juggle several potential solutions.

✓ Are flexible about the solution until a consensus is reached.

✓ Are not "married" to the method and will change approaches if they need to.

Women tend to focus on the "problem" part of problem solving whereas men focus on the "solving." Men roll up their sleeves and tackle a problem in an analytical, linear fashion. Their approach is factual, detached, and action-oriented; their aim is to come up with an action plan quickly. Whereas women's style invites consensus, men's invites debate.

Men thus

✓ Use factual judgment.

✓ Debate.

✓ Stick to the situation at hand.

✓   Think other factors are irrelevant.

✓   Look for "the" solution.

✓   Stick to their solution.

✓   When there's a solution, they consider it "done" and off the list.

The Benefits of Both Approaches

Men's approach to problem solving sets the standard in today's business world, but it has its limitations. Men will benefit if they look for input from their female colleagues who may see other angles of a problem and alternative ways of solving it. This isn't easy for men because it feels like a waste of time and makes them impatient.

By the same token, men's style isn't easy for women. To a lot of women, rolling up your sleeves too early feels like cutting corners. I typically suggest to businesses I consult with that they assign their male and female employees to try each other's styles of problem solving for a week. When they do, they are amazed at the kinds of result they come up with.

Job Interviews

Women usually see job interviews as opportunities for building rapport. Women tend to work very hard on writing their resumes, so they generally assume that theirs will speak for itself. If it lists their accomplishments, women say, why would they have to repeat those accomplishments during their interview? Women don't like blowing their own trumpet. They aren't comfortable bragging about what they've done—because for women, bragging represents behavior they consider tacky.

Typically, men's style in interviews is to promote themselves. Even when their accomplishments are written on a resume, men will repeat the list and expand on each accomplishment in order to demonstrate what they've done in a measurable way. In interviews, they don't hesitate to mention whom they know, and they are quite comfortable taking the credit for achievements—that is, "I was the one who broke last year's sales targets," or "My plan was the break-through idea."

What women will often discuss in an interview is an area of skill or capability they would like to improve. Men, on the other hand, will avoid doing this at all costs. Men will claim ownership of a skill or capability even if it's something they've never tried. They'll sail through the claim, as if were finite and immutable, whereas women will qualify their answers—"I've never really tried that kind of project, but I'm certainly willing to learn." Women will expose vulnerability: for them this is honest and a sign of integrity; it's part of being thorough and balanced; it's more credible; and it demonstrates their ability to be self-critical. Men hide vulnerability at all costs, because for them it's a sign of weakness. For men, it's better to cover up.

Something that interviewers should bear in mind: women are looking for different things in a job from what men seek. Women want to get a feel for the place, for how people interact; they seek to learn what kind of environment it is and whether it suits them. In job interviews, women practice what I call "intuitive judgment." They will check to see if there are other women in the company, what they are doing, what their relationships are with the men they're working for—and with.

Men, on the other hand, are very matter-of-fact in the way they assess a potential job. These are the questions for men: Is this a good strategic move for me? What's my position? What's the salary? Whom will I report to; in other words, where will I be in the hierarchy in this office?

The Benefits of Both Approaches

Different interviewing styles are a huge source of misunderstanding between men and women. Men often assume an accomplished person will have the ego to match the accomplishment. So when women they interview don't show too much ego, men may wonder why they are playing down their accomplishments. Some men even wonder whether those women doctored their resumes. Women, on the other hand, think that if you are accomplished, you can afford to be modest. And they judge men on this. An in-your-face attitude has a real stigma for women. So women will see men as overbearing or unnecessarily boastful.

Imagine the kinds of opportunities that are lost when women and men jump to these conclusions without checking their assumptions first. It's important for both men and women to understand these different styles so that they don't eliminate good candidates because of this misunderstanding.

Performance Evaluations

Most performance evaluations work according to the following logic: "You've accomplished this, but you need to work on that." This doesn't work well for women. They are already critical enough of their own shortcomings. They already have an internal dialogue of struggle going on. Women tend to scrutinize themselves continually. It's part of internalizing things. So pointing out women's weaknesses is not the best way to motivate them. Women need to have their accomplishments clearly articulated. That's what gives them breakthroughs.

Performance evaluations work fine for men because pointing out shortcomings motivates them. One difference is that men don't take evaluations personally as women may do.

The Benefits of Combining Approaches

Men dread giving performance evaluations to women, because they are concerned about how women will react. My advice to men is for them to acknowledge women's strengths, personalize the process by saying, "I really enjoy working with you," and ask women what they think they need to work on next. You'll be surprised. Most of the time, women will bring up the very points you were afraid to deliver yourself. Men will get better results by asking women about their shortcomings instead of telling them what they are.

Men have breakthroughs through hardship, while women have breakthroughs through validation. Men, if you understand the female paradigm, you will have the advantage of being able to promote and validate women, and you'll definitely see the results in women's performance.

Male and Female Behavior at Meetings

We noted earlier that women are comfortable moving away from an agenda. For women, it's part of what you have to do to be thorough. Sometimes the point you have to discuss is so important that it might even change the agenda. This kind of freedom makes room for more voices to be heard. It allows people to bring up new points, other research, or something no one had mentioned—maybe even thought of—before.

Men like to stick to the agenda. To them, it seems like the most efficient way to run a meeting. As we have seen, when women allow the conversation to broaden, men think it's because women lack focus.

Men and women both try to obtain results from meetings. But they use different approaches. Men use an authoritative approach whereas women's traditional approach is to wonder, "What can I do to contribute?" Women often speak in a higher tone of voice, which doesn't project authority as much. Also, unfortunately, the people who speak the loudest are often the ones who are heard.

Being Heard

Women often complain that their ideas aren't "heard." Former U.S. Secretary of State Madeleine Albright once told me that even when she spoke at meetings, her ideas were often ignored; then a man in the meeting would repeat what she had said almost verbatim, and everyone would applaud and tell him he'd made a brilliant point! If it happens to one of the most powerful women I've ever met, it's no surprise it happens to other women.

Men have a style of projecting their voice and sounding determined. In meetings, men tend to take far more air time than women. Women tend to speak in an almost apologetic tone ("Excuse me, if I may…"). I would never ask women to change their natural style; rather, women should learn to frame their contributions by saying,

"I have three things to say; please hear me out." That captures the attention of both men and women. Or perhaps, "I've got this great idea." Women, you shouldn't give yourselves a headache trying to speak louder, but make sure you frame what you say in such a way that people know they're supposed to pay attention: "I want your feedback on this," or, "Hear me out on this." This helps women capture attention in a meeting, and capturing attention is the first step in being heard.

Women should also learn to stand their ground. When there's a lot of controversy or disagreement over a topic, women tend to fold. They make the mistake of thinking that if they have strong feelings about something, the men at the meeting will understand and will take those feelings into consideration. For a woman, the fact that she feels strongly about an issue ought to be enough. But it's not enough. Women have to request very specific actions—"I want this to be done." They need to remember that men will pay attention to the words and the directions women give, but not to the strength of their feelings about the subject. In other words, women need to be clear about what they want.

Selling

Women tend not to sell themselves. What they do is take an interest in their clients. Women cultivate the trust of their clients as a way to build long-term relationships. Statistics show that women are indeed adept at getting repeat business. This means women can walk out of a sales situation empty-handed but still feel that they've achieved something. The "win" for women is to build rapport with clients and get results.

The "win" for men is closing the sale. They get satisfaction when they go in with an objective and come out with a result.

Women are better at reading people, so, for example, they'll read when a sale is not going well and will be able to change gear, offer another project, or ask the client open-ended questions about "something else that might be more suitable." Women make connections to people, whereas men make object-focused connections to stories—like the story of a conquest.

The Benefits of Combining Approaches

The ideal sales team has built-in gender balance so it can apply both approaches. Studies show that women are as good at reading men as they are at reading women, while men are only good at reading men. So men should look to their female colleagues for insight on women.

When men and women go on joint sales calls, they should be ready to use either or both of the approaches, depending on the client. With their strict focus on results, men risk missing important details about a client's expectations or needs. Let women lead the way on this, and they'll work it out in no time. The real challenge is for both men and women is to avoid stepping on each other's toes. If they can evaluate a client's needs and expectations, they can let the person with the most effective technique take the lead.

Men should just bear in mind that "closing the sale" is not the only thing that's important to women. And women should bear in mind that for men, it is.

Delegating

Women tend to have a hard time delegating. They take on a lot at work, then get bogged down in detail work or by doing research they could hand over to someone else. The result? Women often feel overwhelmed and overworked.

Men are more comfortable delegating tasks to others. They also have a strong ability to simplify things. They'll slim things down, consolidating numerous items into just a few. Women are more trusting about sharing information than are men, but when it comes to workload, they are not as comfortable handing work over, especially the "grunt work." It's the methodology of it, really. Men have an easier time handing over work, probably because they are socialized to give orders.

In cross-mentoring, women find that when they are mentored by a man in this area, they learn to delegate better.

The Benefits of Combining Approaches

Women can learn a lot from men. They should look at the way men comfortably make requests of others. To women, this feels like asking others to do their work for them. But it's not. In most cases, things can be simplified and women can greatly reduce their workload while still achieving good results. When women emulate men's delegation style, they are surprised what a load it takes off their shoulders.

Negotiation

Women have an ability to negotiate in an inclusive way. They naturally tend to hear everyone out. Studies have shown that women retain this ability even in crisis situations. Women use "exploring ideas" as a form of negotiation, often by asking the parties to consider a different way of looking at the issue. This style has the effect of making people pause and relax, and that, in turn, often opens them up to compromise. Women are sociologically brought up to be peacemakers. They validate situations so people feel heard. They defuse the debate.

Women will

✓ Ask open-ended questions like "How do you feel about this?"

✓ Keep the tone collegial while they build the relationship and make it stronger.

✓ Use a collaborative style, saying "Let's explore this."

✓ Validate the other's position. "You look at it that way. I look at it this way."

✓ Show flexibility.

✓ Look for a collaborative, flexible, win-win solution. They will give and take.

Men tend to escalate the debate. They tend to play devil's advocate and approach negotiation in a linear way. They treat it as a seesaw process. "I make my demands, the other party makes its demands, and eventually we agree on something." Men see negotiating as a matter of competing for position. They go in with a goal in mind and drive to achieve it.

Men will

✓ Use action-oriented, closed questions, like "What do you want?"

✓ Speak in finite terms about what they've agreed on; for example, they'll say, "So far we've decided this."

✓ Look for closure.

✓ Use an argumentative style.

✓ Show consistency.

✓ Agree to disagree.

The Benefits of Combining Approaches

Like selling, negotiating is a fine art. Different countries and cultures have their own rules. So it's good to enter negotiations with as many strategies at your disposal as possible. Women's style achieves results too—often better results. But sometimes men's approach is more effective. Men and women negotiating together should be aware of their different styles and be willing to adapt to the circumstances they find themselves in. Sometimes sticking to your own demands is a good idea. But sometimes the more explorative approach is better. Men and women can easily learn their respective styles by watching each other negotiate in different circumstances.

Networking

For women, networking is a good opportunity to build ongoing relationships and lasting support bases. Women feel a sense of bonding when they're networking. They'll stay in a group for a long time instead of skipping from one person to the next. Women often network with no particular objective in mind. They feel it's rude and even tacky to network in a self-serving and transparent manner.

Women will

✓ Use "web" thinking; they create a series of networks that interconnect.

✓ Constantly nurture those networks, even though it's not an evident means to a specific end.

✓ Often just have a hunch that something fruitful will come out of a relationship.

✓ Will juggle relationships that don't necessarily have anything to do with one another.

✓ Often network just to learn something new.

Men move around a lot when they are in a networking situation. For them, networking is usually done with a specific purpose in mind. It's a means to an end. Men want to meet specific contacts for specific reasons.

Men will

✓ Become members of clubs either for status or to get connections as a means to a specific end.

✓ Cultivate a variety of networks: they have friends with whom they socialize, others with whom they enjoy recreation, and others who may enhance their results in business.

Both women's and men's networks are "fluid"; that is, a new contact is often introduced to an existing network acquaintance, who may then add the new "name" to his or her own network. In the existing setup, however, men tend to network with men and therefore don't get to know women. That means that when it's time to suggest individuals for promotion, men don't have the criteria for judging women's potential. All they can do is look at women's accomplishments.

How do you solve this situation? Men don't need to leave the networks they have, but they should either invite women into those networks or learn to go out of their comfort zone into networks where there are more women. That's the only way men will get to know women and understand the unique strengths women bring to business. Men should take their cue from women's approach to networking: network to learn, rather than to achieve specific goals. You will achieve the goal of getting to know talented women.

The Benefits of Combining Approaches

Men and women can both learn from watching each other network. Because of their open-ended networking style, women sometimes lose out on great opportunities. They are afraid of appearing too purposeful when they meet people. But women can shed some of that hesitation by watching a male colleague work a room. Of course, men's results-driven networking style means they run the risk of alienating people—especially women. By watching women network, men can pick up tips for building rapport and long-term relationships. Sometimes these things are more valuable than short-term results.

One more hint to both genders: women continue networking by maintaining personal contact with others, sending a personal message via e-mail or voicemail every so often, making a useful introduction. Men usually stay in touch by sending things: documents, newspaper articles, or web links. Women should not be offended if the men they network with don't phone them. That's what men are doing by sending an interesting article. But men should remember that personal communications with women will go a long way in solidifying the relationship. It doesn't take much effort, and the results last forever.

Public Speaking

Women tend to approach speaking engagements as dialogues. They often appear to audiences more as facilitators than as presenters. Women are not comfortable "pontificating" when they speak. Rather, they tend to invite listeners to participate and ask questions. They like to be inviting and encourage dialogue when they speak.

Men usually follow the traditional "declarative" style of public speaking: articulate an argument, restate it, summarize it, wrap it up, and then wait for the applause. Men tend to want to keep questions under control. They'd rather get people to subscribe to their argument than solicit feedback on it.

There is a stereotypical assumption about what makes a good public speaker: a convincing, authoritative storyteller who is in control of the audience. That tends to be more of a male approach. The snag is that women who conform to this approach are interpreted as being too forceful, unapproachable, and arrogant. The women who have established themselves—who are powerful, well-known experts or "celebrities"—are freed from this and can express themselves authentically. They are seen as engaging and inquisitive, and they stimulate dialogue; they "ask more rather than tell more," and are "humorous" as opposed to "telling jokes."

What can the average woman do to break out of this syndrome of not being taken seriously? Women are certainly articulate, and this is the attribute they need to use to establish their own credibility. Not through male "style" but through authentic engagement with the audience—by asserting her experience or the indisputability of her argument—will a woman capture the attention of her audience and lay the groundwork for her own authentic, inquisitive speaking style.

The Benefits of Combining Approaches

If you want to have a participatory event, where people will listen and feel comfortable giving their points of view, you had better get a woman to design it. It's worth taking the time to decide what kind of presentation you want to deliver. Studies show that people are tired of the traditional presentation style in which they are "talked at." It means that men can learn a lot from women's approach to making presentations and speeches.

You may have heard the old saying: "When men speak, people listen. When women speak, people look. If they like what they see, they listen." Unfortunately, in today's business world, this still holds true. So women have to go the extra distance to establish credibility when they speak. Women's natural, participatory public speaking style may not help them in all situations, and where it won't work, they would do well to watch men's style. Both genders should gauge the nature of the presentation they have to make and take their cues from each other.

Look to the Other

As is obvious by now, combining approaches is a key way to optimize the synergy that can be gained from the separate strengths of each gender's different approach. I learned about the advantage of combining men and women's perspectives firsthand with a former client. Looking back on it now, this personal breakthrough had a huge influence on my life. It is one of the reasons I do the work I do today.

It all started with one relatively small incident. I had been working for months on a sales contract for the client. At first I thought I had a great relationship with the client team, but over time, I began to doubt this. The more work I did, the more the team asked me to do extra work that wasn't part of our contract. One day, my frustration reached the boiling point, so I went looking for some sympathy from one of my male colleagues. I was starting to feel genuinely frustrated by this client's behavior. "Why would they think they could take advantage of me that way?" I asked him.

My colleague's assessment of the situation, coming from his male perspective, reflected a completely different perspective. I was looking for sympathy, but what I got was a solution. "Maybe they're not deliberately taking advantage of you," my colleague offered. "Maybe they just love your work. Instead of getting frustrated with your client, why don't you just go back to the contract and try to make an amendment so that you will be compensated for your extra time?" I acted on his advice and faxed the amended contract to the client with my request. The client team agreed to my terms. I solved the problem in half an hour and probably saved weeks or even months of self-questioning. It probably saved my relationship with that client too.

Sometimes getting an opinion from a member of the other gender can be very helpful. Both women and men would gain a lot from following this advice. The fact that men don't tend to take things as personally can be a boost when women want a different perspective on a problem. I often turn to male colleagues and associates when I'm feeling overwhelmed by the implications of a problem. Quite often, they help me stop ruminating and start looking for solutions.

There are also lots of ways women's viewpoints can help men deal with a problem. A former client tells me he never makes major decisions now without consulting at least two women. "Women's multi-thinking often helps me see all the implications of a problem, so I can judge better if a solution is going to be effective," he says.

Clients who have participated in this work often call me up to tell me stories of breakthroughs they had when they got a new perspective from a male or female colleague. One man, a manager at an investment firm, says women's input saved him from a very big mistake. There were two women on his advisory board when he was approached by a technology start-up company looking for financing. The company wined and dined him and presented a thorough business plan. He was sold on the idea, but the two women on his board were hesitant. They told him they had a feeling there was something wrong. They couldn't put their finger on it exactly, but something in the story of the relationship the company had with other firms didn't add up. The other men on the board said, "It's not an issue." But my client wisely gave the women the time to follow their hunch.

The technology company had emphasized the number of contracts they already had with major companies, but something in their language sounded vague. The women decided to telephone all the other companies to see if the tech company was really working for them. It turned out that contracts for eight of the ten projects in their business plan had not actually been signed. Women's "exploratory" thinking saved this firm a lot of money.

In another story, a member of a law society told me about the society's project to locate firms with exemplary gender equality records in order to promote this among their members. The society automatically focused on large law firms, thinking people would pay more attention to these firms. But several women involved in the project—those who had done their homework—pointed out that 90 percent of law firms are actually small. Therefore, the women argued, examples of small firms that excelled in gender equality would be more meaningful to the majority of law firms—and the majority of lawyers.

But of course, the road runs in two directions. Women's multithinking can lead them to situations where they can't see their way out of problems. Pondering over problems and revisiting them can bring new angles that lead to solutions but can also make problems seem overwhelmingly complex. Typically, when women find themselves in this situation, they turn to colleagues for advice. Actually, they contact them in order to "talk about it." If those colleagues are men, they tend to respond with solutions. And as we have seen, solutions often backfire on women. Women interpret men's behavior as dismissive.

I recommend that women anticipate the type of reaction they'll get from men and mine the gold. Women have to remember that when men give solutions, they are giving what is, in their terms, their best effort. A men's perspective can help women stop pondering over problems and act when it's time to act.

Be More Inclusive: Start with Giving Promotions

We tend to promote people who are like us and only to promote people who are unlike us when they emulate us. This goes for both men and women—except that until recently, men have done most of the promoting in the working world. The result was a pattern where men promoted men on their potential but only promoted women for their accomplishments. Men don't do this deliberately. It's about their "comfort zone."

As we've noted, men tend to network with men, so they don't get to know women very well. But men don't need to leave the comfort of their networks to change this situation; rather, they should either invite women into their networks or learn to go out of their comfort zone into networks where there are more women. That's the only way men will get to know women and understand the unique strengths women bring to business.

The challenge for all businesses and individual managers is to learn to be more inclusive, not only in employing people, but also in giving promotions. And the way to do that is to expand your ideas about what qualities employees need to be "right" for the job. When you are taking someone on, scrutinize your decisions to see if you are choosing the person who is most like you or the person who is best for the job. We are all limiting ourselves by promoting "likeness." As you have seen, there is strength in difference.

Converting Differences into Strengths

The truth is, we can no longer afford to work in the traditional business model we saw in Chapter 1. We created a machine that worked well in the past but simply doesn't work anymore. Businesses need to learn to be flexible and understand how men and women are different. And then they need to use those differences to their advantage.

For the most part, this means including the attributes women bring to the workplace instead of seeing those qualities as obstacles. Daniel Goleman, author of *Emotional Intelligence*, makes the point that we create business from an old paradigm.[1] His argument is that typical female attributes are more necessary than ever in today's business environment in which, to get ahead, we rely less on linear, analytical thinking and more on emotional intelligence.

This chart summarizes men and women's different strengths.

Women	Men
Rapport talk	Report talk
Collaborative	Competitive
Suggestive	Directive
Internalize	Externalize
Connected	Detached
Contextual	Specific
Flexible	Consistent
Intuitive	Factual
Network for relationships	Network for connections
Validate	Debate

What we have to do is look for the approach that is appropriate and effective for different circumstances. Historically, we've depended on the right side of the chart. When women entered the workplace, we tried to clone those "right side" qualities onto both genders. What a waste of skills and talents! If you choose to draw from both sides of the chart, you'll be amazed at the kinds of breakthroughs you'll achieve, both personally and for your company.

Things Are Changing

I'm happy to report that many companies have learned to put the strengths of both genders to work for them. And the result for

---

1. Daniel Goleman, *Emotional Intelligence: Why It Can Matter More Than IQ* (New York: Bantam Books, 2005).

them was that the environment changed, and the individuals in it flourished. Changing the work environment so it suits everyone is a big job, and a long-term commitment, but I can feel the change at many of the companies I have worked with. Before organizations start working on gender awareness, the men working there tend to be guarded. The women feel they have to struggle to be taken seriously. After the organizations have made a serious commitment to gender intelligence, their working environments become inviting, collaborative, and enjoyable.

I have particularly noticed changes in sales and consulting businesses I have worked with. In many of these companies the macho boardroom environment has just vanished. What I see in its place is a culture of "clusters," where coworkers team up to work on problems collaboratively. One company has introduced formal brainstorming sessions. The rule is that anyone—including new employees—can take the floor, talk about a problem, give advice, and say what's on his or her mind. In a genuinely collaborative atmosphere, people feel comfortable and speak up. And sometimes they have brilliant ideas.

One small change in an investment firm struck me as particularly significant. I recall that the first time I visited the firm, its cafeteria was strictly segregated: there was one long table for senior management, and no one else sat at it, even if it was empty. The last time I visited the company, the table was gone. Everyone was making an effort to sit with someone new every day. The president told me he sits down to eat with the janitor every now and again, "just to see what's going on."

I invite companies to try to get a discussion going about gender difference. Some companies have found some truly ingenious ways to do this. One firm started a cross-gender mentoring and "buddy" system. When employees need a new perspective on an issue, they call up their buddy: men and women interact by e-mail, phone, or by having lunch together. They bounce ideas, problems, and business challenges off each other and find that—in a casual and informal way—this exchange of views from different angles enhances their work. They also learn how to communicate more effectively with the other gender. Mentoring, on the other hand, is hierarchically structured, because the mentor is an experienced and more senior employee.

Some companies have ongoing cross-gender lunches where employees can exchange perspectives and talk about gender difference. One president I know systematically consults a senior female executive and a female middle manager before he makes decisions—just to get their insights and opinions.

If you are a manager or supervisor, the important thing to understand is that in order to make change, you've got to mean it. Women have a perception that gender equality is just the flavor of the month. They believe their companies are addressing gender issues because everyone else is, or because they want to project an image of being a progressive, people-friendly place to work. These women don't believe the will to change is really there.

It is essential to turn a no-win situation into a win-win situation. Gaining gender intelligence will make everyone happier and feel valued. Deep down, that's what everyone wants. Unfortunately, there are some obstacles that may still prevent companies from reaching this goal. In the next chapter, we'll look at how conflicts unfold, and how you can avoid and overcome such situations.

10

Resolving Gender Conflicts

What matters most is how we respond to what we experience in life.

—Viktor Frankl, author, *Man's Search for Meaning*

Men and women have different styles and approaches to most of the tasks we perform in an average working day. Once you understand these differences, you can easily turn them to your advantage. But when it comes to workplace conflicts, we tend to lose sight of this strength in being different.

Part of the problem is that when it comes to conflict, men and women come from two different worlds. Women see conflict as a breakdown. They view it as corrosive. One reason for this is that women internalize, and the conflict automatically becomes personal. For men, conflict is not so much a breakdown as a struggle. Men tend to react to conflict as if it were a challenge, a contest to be won. It's a call to battle.

Men and women don't deal with conflict the same way either. Women's first reaction to conflict is to personalize it. They wonder, "What did I do?" Men tend to treat conflict in an isolated, depersonalized manner. For women, it's about the relationship. That's one reason women tend to approach a conflict by treating it as an opportunity, a chance to clear up and clear away issues, build rapport, and strengthen the relationship. Women's instinct is to explore a conflict, figuring out how the conflict or its solution might affect other parties. Women ask others to get to the bottom of the problem by sharing their feelings. Men, on the other hand, tend to react to conflict by staking out a position—much the way they do when they negotiate. At work, they typically bark orders to others in a directive, here's-what-we're-going-to-do manner.

What do men and women in conflict have in common? Conflicts always start at the same source: unmet expectations. When our expectations are not met—for example, when someone hasn't done the job he or she promised to do or the one we expected—we are surprised. The impact of the unfulfilled promise hits us, and we have a reaction: frustration, uncertainty, anger, all of the above. Men and women both go through this basic reaction to conflict. It's almost universal. But after that, men and women head off in 'different directions.

We all know what those directions are. Men typically explode. They instinctively, instantly look outside to someone or something else. They'll show anger and direct it at that something or someone. They'll slam their fist on a table or yell. It's the way they let their stress out.

Women usually find this reaction perplexing—even frightening. But that's because women's own way of reacting to conflict is almost the opposite. Women implode. When they find themselves in a conflict, the first question women tend to ask is, "What have I done wrong?" This doesn't mean they aren't angry. Women hold their reaction inside themselves while they try to make sense of it. They're working on their reaction internally. They ponder, mull it over—even if it's only briefly. Then they may have an emotional reaction, sometimes to the point of crying. Men find this perplexing because they think tears are a sign of sadness. They often tell me tears make them feel helpless. But, as we've seen, tears, at work, are almost always an expression of frustration and anger.

Many experts in different disciplines see these basic differences in different terms. Linguist Walter Ong points out in *Fighting for Life* that men's reaction to conflict is part of a set of ritualized behaviors that includes contests, competition, struggle, and contention.[1] Paleopsychologist Howard Bloom, author of *Global Brain*,[2] writes that in organizations, men spend more time posturing, or in hierarchical displays or territorial competitions. When women deal with conflicts, he writes, they "dig in, find solutions and get back to work."

---

1. Walter J. Ong, *Fighting for Life: Contest, Sexuality, and Consciousness* (Ithaca, NY: Cornell University Press, 1981).

2. Howard Bloom, *Global Brain: The Evolution of Mass Mind from the Big Bang to the 21st Century* (New York: Wiley, 2001).

So although women may be less purely results-oriented than men are in many aspects of working life, when it comes to conflict, Bloom says they are "more goal-oriented and less political."

Attacking versus Resolving

It's not that women are afraid of conflict. They just don't like conflict for conflict's sake. Working women often ask me, "Why do we have to have all this debate at the office all the time?" Women see debate and arguing as "attacking." Women also say they find men locked into their position or inflexible when they deal with conflicts. But that's because women assume, from the start, that the way to solve conflicts is through conciliation. For women, winning is not usually the real point.

Linguist Deborah Tannen, in her book *The Argument Culture*, writes that women at work are frequently puzzled by how men can argue with each other and then continue as if nothing has happened.[3] Men at work are often surprised when women are deeply upset by a verbal attack. For men, it's simply part of getting the job done. But women often wonder, "Why does he have to jump all over me like that?" It is common for men to use ritual opposition even where there is no real conflict; such behaviors include teasing, playfully insulting each other, and exploring ideas by playing devil's advocate. This approach creates tension and conflict between women and men at work. Many women avoid overt disagreement when they really do disagree, because conflict for them signals a breakdown.

According to psychologists John Gottman and Robert Levenson at the University of Washington, you can see the differences in how men and women react to conflict by simply observing the physiological changes conflict provokes. The pair asked male and female patients to identify and discuss a major area of disagreement in their marriage. While the patients were doing this, the researchers monitored such factors as the subjects' heart rates, blood flow, skin temperature, and body movements. What did they find?

---

3. Deborah Tannen, *The Argument Culture: Stopping America's War of Words* (New York: Ballantine Books, 1999).

Men literally get more "heated up" and physically stimulated by conflict. Women experience less physical change during sustained conflict. Their conclusion? Men need to shut off or cool down during conflict, or they get overwhelmed and lose control, whereas women can tolerate longer, escalating bouts of conflict without losing control.

So How Can We Resolve Conflicts?

Most of us know how to resolve conflicts. We get advice like "Explain your viewpoint" or "Be very clear, consistent, and direct." Most of us go through our careers assuming that this is all there is to do. And we think it's probably enough. Of course, if we look around and make a tally of the number of continuing conflicts we see or hear about in an average week at the office, we might start to wonder just how efficient these good old methods for solving conflicts really are.

I can tell you—from the number of conflicts I'm called in to deal with in an average week— that the good old methods don't work. And they don't work because we all overlook a few basic things about the nature of conflicts.

We've seen in previous chapters how men and women each assume that the other gender thinks like they do. So they project their own reactions onto those of the other gender. In conflict, men and women do the same thing: they assume the other gender hears the same words and speaks the same language as they do. But of course, men and women don't speak the same language. Their words and actions don't necessarily mean the same thing. So, unless you recognize how your actions appear to the other gender, your reaction will only make things worse.

This syndrome of misunderstandings is as common at work as it is at home. One of my associates, Emily, told me this story of a typical conflict she and her husband got into over cooking together. Their kitchen is small, so it isn't easy to cook together, but that day, things were going particularly smoothly. Then, according to Brenda, "Andrew hit his head by accident on a cupboard door. And how did he react? He slammed the cupboard door shut so hard the glass broke!" Like most women, Emily took her husband's expression of

Emily & Andrew cooking together.

anger personally. It felt like an attack on her, one that shattered the feeling of harmony in the narrow kitchen into as many pieces as the shards of glass from the cupboard door. Equally, Emily was mystified. To her, Andrew's reaction seemed completely out of proportion to the accident—which was just a result of his own carelessness. "Why does he have to take out his anger on a cupboard door?" The way she saw it, Andrew had stolen a good moment from her. They were cooking peacefully and he went and ruined it by overreacting to what looked like a pretty minor incident to her. She told him what she thought.

Andrew simply didn't understand why Emily was hurt and offended by his outburst. He told her it was just his way of letting off steam. "It's got nothing to do with you," he said. But to Emily, it did have something to do with her. She persisted in resenting his reaction. This left Andrew confused and frustrated. They both felt misunderstood. She was stuck in her position—"You overreacted"—and he was stuck in his—"It had nothing to do with you." And by that point, neither of them felt like being in the same room, let alone cooking together in a tiny kitchen.

men explode
women implode

This is a classic dynamic between men and women in conflict. The more men explode, the more women implode. When women personalize situations, men's frustration meter rises; they feel they're being accused of something they didn't intend. "It's not about you." When women hear this, they tend to shut down because they also feel they're not being understood.

Boss wasn't attacking

It happens at work all the time. One of my clients, <u>Alexis</u>, called me with a typical male-female work conflict situation. She was convinced that her <u>boss, Ray,</u> was being abusive toward her. By the time she called me, she was on the verge of hiring a lawyer to sue him. I asked her where this feeling came from. "In almost every e-mail he sends he clearly appears to me to be angry!" Alexis felt that the e-mails were attacks. I suspected she was misinterpreting Ray's style, so I asked her if I could read them myself. The style of the e-mails was clearly "directive" and abrupt, but all it took was a brief conversation with her boss for Alexis to realize her assumption had been dead wrong. <u>Ray wasn't attacking</u> her. It was a matter of style; his was directive, and she took it as abusive. A way of writing aimed at managing

His manage style is direct

or guiding an operation somehow sounded disparaging to her. In just one quick meeting, she and her boss resolved the misunderstanding.

E-mails can be a major cause of communication breakdown as our dependence on digital communication grows. Try to avoid having an argument this way—one that is meticulously documented and that you may regret.

Pick up the telephone before the situation can escalate. The challenge in conflicts—as in all your dealings with the opposite gender—is to avoid becoming a victim of your own faulty assumptions. To avoid this fate, the first thing you need is S.A.R.A.

S.A.R.A.

I learned a great lesson about how we react to conflict situations from a famous psychologist I once studied with, Virginia Satir. She said that people go through four stages when they are in a conflict: Surprise, Anger, Rejection, and Acceptance.[4] Some people go through every stage. Others skip some stages. Some people are surprised but go straight to Acceptance without passing through Anger. These are all normal human reactions and are nothing to be ashamed about. In fact, it's better to have these reactions and recognize them for what they are than to pretend you don't have them. You'll soon see why.

Without realizing it, most people get stuck in either Anger or Rejection. Where you get stuck partly depends on gender. Men tend to get stuck in Anger, projecting their reaction to conflict in an outward direction. Not surprisingly, women tend to get stuck in Rejection, because they project their reaction to conflict inward, incorporating the rejection into their sense of themselves.

The problem is that when men are stuck in Anger and women are stuck in Rejection, their reactions reinforce one another. Perceptual filters kick in again. In Rejection, women say, "I feel unheard." This triggers men's anger because men feel they're being blamed. When men react defensively, they retrigger women's feeling of rejection.

---

4. Virginia Satir, *Peoplemaking* (Palo Alto, CA: Science and Behavior Books, Inc., 1972).

That makes women feel men don't want to listen to them, which feeds that feeling of being unheard even more.

This syndrome, in which men's and women's reactions reinforce each other, doesn't help the ultimate problem both genders face: getting to Acceptance. Why is this so important? When we are stuck in Surprise, Anger, or Rejection, it is too early to act. You can't do anything productive to resolve a conflict in these stages. That's why it's good to recognize the stages. Once you have, you need to take whatever time you need to get to Acceptance.

Commit to Short-Term Suffering

Getting to Acceptance is a matter of intentions. I often tell people, "It can take five minutes or it can take five years. You decide. But it has to be done." How do you get to Acceptance? The best way is to remind yourself of your long-term intentions. Our long-term intentions are the first thing we forget about when we're in a conflict. But they're usually more important than being "right." That means you have to accept some short-term suffering.

A young accountant, David, told me a story that perfectly illustrates why it's so important to get over Anger and Rejection before doing anything about a conflict. Many people will relate to this phone message scenario. David was head of a team of 18 accountants working on a tax return for a large company. While he was on a business trip, his team leader left him three messages warning him that they were probably not going to make the deadline. The team was having difficulty getting needed information from the client. On his way back from his trip, David picked up one last message from his voicemail. This time it was from the client. The president accused David of being unprofessional because David's team was clearly behind schedule. "We are one of your largest clients," he said on the voicemail message. "And this shows us we're not really that important to you."

"I was stunned," David recalled. "I knew it wasn't our fault, and it certainly wasn't my fault! I remember I was on the sidewalk holding my cell phone, pacing back and forth. Then I just hit the callback button and unloaded on his voicemail. It was a knee-jerk reaction."

As soon as David ended the call he knew he had made a mistake. "I thought about it for a second and realized there was probably a misunderstanding. There was probably a communication problem somewhere. I wished so much I could get into the president's voicemail and delete my message."

It turned out that a communication problem *was* at the root of the misunderstanding. In his attempt to get the required information from the client, the team leader had left repeated messages—with no response. The reason was that the client staff was busy getting the information together, and it was taking longer than they expected. But David didn't know that. Neither did the company's president. And company staff were so involved in gathering the needed information they neglected to respond to the increasingly insistent messages from David's team. Bottom line: accountant and client each saw the delay and automatically assumed it was the other's fault. "It wasn't really anyone's fault," David said.

There are two ways of dealing with conflicts: what I call the Blame Frame and the Outcome Frame. We tend to fall into the Blame Frame before we get to Acceptance, and it is a win-lose mindset. When you are in Blame Frame, you are attached to your opinion. You are attached to being right. Your objective is to prove the other person wrong.

By contrast, when you are in the Outcome Frame, your goal is to find real resolution. Your objective is to find a win-win solution that will make everyone happy.

Lots of people in conflict think it is unrealistic to have a win-win solution. They think somebody has to lose. That's just because they are in the Blame Frame.

When you are in Surprise, Anger, or Rejection, you're probably operating in the Blame Frame, and when you're in the Blame Frame, it's too early to act. Blaming is a normal human reaction. No one likes conflicts, and when they happen, the first thing we think about is ourselves. We want to pin the fault on someone else. But that's the problem with trying to resolve a conflict when you are in the Blame Frame. It's about fault-finding, not solution-finding. It's about "you or me." It's zero-sum, win or lose, "I'm right and you're wrong." Most people assume you solve conflicts by talking. But talking won't solve anything if you're in the Blame Frame. It only digs you deeper. You're still trying to decide who is at fault.

David's story is a perfect example. David was in Blame Frame when he made the snap decision to call the president and unload on him. When David felt attacked, he reacted by attacking back. He may have felt momentary relief after speaking his mind to the president's voicemail, but that didn't do much to solve the problem. He understood that pretty quickly.

After David left the first message, he cooled down a bit, got over his Anger, and decided to look for a win-win solution. David was in Acceptance. He was ready for the Outcome Frame. He started by checking his assumptions. He made a few calls to find out how the misunderstanding had occurred. He quickly realized that everyone was acting in good faith. So he called the president back and explained the situation. They agreed it was no one's fault and extended the deadline for the tax return. Problem solved.

The Win-Win Way—Outcome Frame

The only way to resolve a conflict is to change from the Blame Frame to the Outcome Frame. This means switching your frame of reference from fault-finding to solution-finding. These five tips will help you:

1. **Take a break.** Remove yourself. "I'll get back to you on that" is a magic formula for taking yourself out of the equation. Personally, I give myself five minutes to do this. I do it on my own. You can also go and see someone else, if you need to.

2. If you do choose to see someone else, **make sure that person is a committed listener, not just an "ear."** If you're looking for someone you can rely on for sympathy, you'll end up stuck back in the Blame Frame. It's sensible to choose someone with a completely differently perspective from your own, maybe even someone you don't know that well. Present that person with your challenge and explain what you're looking for.

3. **Get in touch with your long-term intentions.** Are you committed to working with this client/colleague/partner? Do you

want to make a partnership or collaboration work? If the answer is yes, then you need to ask a few simple questions. How can we resolve this? What would be an ideal solution for you?

4. **Forget about who's right and who's wrong and focus on the cost of the conflict.** To do so, you have to be in Acceptance. You have to get over "being right."

5. **Detach yourself from your opinions,** because the first step in resolving conflicts through the Outcome Frame is to find out what a "winning" solution would be for the other side.

When you follow these basic steps, your hostilities usually melt away, and the solution will follow.

The following story of a conflict at an engineering firm shows how you can move from the Blame Frame to the Outcome Frame—and how easy it is to find a solution once you're in the Outcome Frame. The story involved two colleagues, Gordon, a partner at the firm, and Megan, the accounts manager.

Gordon had received a call from one of the firm's most important clients; the caller insisted that his company needed a contract finished for the next day. Gordon was still feeling the shock of that when he went to talk to Megan at 3 p.m. "It absolutely has to be done for tomorrow," he said. "We don't have a choice." That really put Megan on the spot. She had promised her husband she would pick up the children from childcare that afternoon at 5 p.m. "I'll work on it for the next two hours, but I absolutely have to be away by 5 p.m.," she said.

Gordon's reaction? "It absolutely has to be done by tomorrow."

Megan was shocked but she tried a compromise. "I'll try to get a babysitter, and if I can, I'll come back tonight and work on it. But I can't make any promises," she said.

That just made Gordon angrier. He blurted out in frustration, "Oh, not the children again! It's just impossible for it to wait. I promised it would be on the client's desk tomorrow morning."

The sarcastic comment about her children really hurt Megan. Gordon's words put her on the defensive. I label conflicts like Megan's and Gordon's as the jugular variety. They get people by the throat—the jugular—by dragging up sensitive issues. They aren't easy to defuse. They bring out emotions we didn't know we had, and they trigger reactions we're not even aware of.

But even these kinds of conflict can be solved by switching from the Blame Frame to the Outcome Frame. Gordon was stuck in Anger and Megan was stuck in feeling Rejection. After they got over their reactions and got into Acceptance, they were able to move toward finding a solution. Gordon started by taking ownership of his request. He told Megan, "I am having a huge problem with this client. They absolutely insist on having this contract done by tomorrow morning, and I promised they would have it. Is there a way we can meet this deadline?" *Problem-solving outcome mode.*

Megan dropped her defenses. Gordon's approach put her in a problem-solving, outcome mode. Megan knew the client. She knew it was a company that often made these kinds of last-minute demands. And she knew that after they got their contracts, they let them sit for three weeks before they did anything with them. She explained this to Gordon. "I know this client makes a lot of demands. But I also know that if I push, they'll give a bit. It usually doesn't turn out to be a problem when we can't do things as quickly as they want."

When Gordon heard this he understood something about his earlier reaction to the client's request. He explained to Megan that he was from the old school, where the customer is king. Megan explained her point of view. She said that her team would do a better job if they had a reasonable amount of time. "The overall outcome will be better," she said. They agreed that if she worked a few hours from home over the weekend, then finished the rest early in the week, without rushing the job, the client would probably be happier. They were right; the client was well pleased with the quality of the work.

Team Conflicts

An office equipment company once approached me for advice on how to deal with another of these "jugular" conflicts among three of its sales representatives. The conflict started when the three—two women, Caroline and Grace, and one man, Greg—went to make a presentation to a potential client. The stakes were high. The contract was one of the biggest the company had ever seen. Greg made the presentation, and they lost the contract. That's when the conflict started. Grace and Caroline blamed Greg for blowing it.

Greg didn't think it was his fault. He said he gave it his best effort. In Greg's version of events, he was making a presentation to the senior executive, a man, and three women who worked for the senior manager. Greg just followed his instinct. Without even thinking about it, he zeroed in on the male manager. Later, Greg reported, "I just gave him the facts. I told him we had the best product at the best price and that he was guaranteed satisfaction. And I did a great job." Greg didn't have a clue about what went wrong.

But Grace and Caroline certainly did! They said Greg had started going downhill the minute he opened his mouth. "It was obviously the women who were making the decision," they explained. "And Greg didn't pay much attention to them." Their competitors took a much softer approach to the sale, and Grace and Caroline could see it was working.

"You blew it," they told Greg after the presentations. Greg wouldn't hear of it. "No. I did a terrific job!"

The team lost the sale, but that wasn't the real problem. The real problem was that the incident sparked a conflict between the team members that no one seemed able to resolve. That was when their sales director came to see me.

The first thing I did was listen to everyone's version of events. Grace and Caroline said that right from the start they had seen Greg's approach wasn't working. "You came across as overbearing and condescending," they told him. "The women in the room could tell that the only one you thought you had to convince was their boss, and they were turned off." Greg reacted defensively. "You can't blame *me*. I did a perfect job." He said that he thought everyone was plotting against him. Grace and Caroline said he refused to listen to them. They were in a deadlock.

Their dispute shows how easy it is to fall into the Blame Frame. "We saw that Greg was losing the client right away," they told me. "After that, we just saw a checklist of what was going wrong, of the mistakes he was making." In other words, Grace's and Caroline's Blame Frame shaped the way they saw Greg's whole presentation.

Greg was in the Blame Frame too. He said his only thought about the whole incident was that "Grace and Caroline are ganging up on me." He felt like a victim, as if they were gathering evidence against him. "It's not my fault. It's their fault." And what did he do? He stopped listening to them. He shut down. Grace and Caroline, meanwhile, assumed Greg just wasn't listening. Their reactions reinforced one another.

There isn't much you can do to avoid going through the Blame Frame. It's all part of the normal human reaction to conflict situations. The problem is that when you are in the Blame Frame, you aren't ready to do anything to really resolve a conflict. You can't resolve conflicts when you are focused on having your own position understood. What you have to be able to say is this: "I want to understand the other person."

Greg, Grace, and Caroline had to wait a few weeks before they were ready to move from the Blame Frame to the Outcome Frame. How did they do this? They started by recalling what their long-term goals were. As I've said before, the first thing that goes out of the window when we are in a conflict are our long-term intentions. As soon as Greg and Grace and Caroline were in a conflict situation, they forgot they were a good team.

Lost of trust & special team dynamics

I asked them, "What's the cost of being in the Blame Frame?" It didn't take them long to come up with an answer. They lost trust in one another, they said. And they lost the special chemistry that had made them a good team. As they would later see, being in the Blame Frame was probably what lost them their client too. "What are you all committed to?" I asked them. Again, it didn't take them long to come up with an answer. "Being a strong team. That's how we win clients," they answered. When they all heard themselves saying the same thing, the dispute suddenly went from "it's you against me" to "it's you *and* me."

Long term intents? good team

That's when Greg, Grace, and Caroline switched from the Blame Frame to the Outcome Frame. Then the past event took on a whole new meaning for them. They all saw what they could have done to save the situation. "I have a confession to make," said Caroline. "I knew the women in the room would have the last word on the purchase. I could have jumped in and steered your attention to them. But instead, I just watched your presentation ticking like a time bomb." In the Blame Frame, Greg saw that he would have closed the door on that kind of interruption. But in the Outcome Frame, he would have welcomed it. He would have realized Caroline had a reason for doing what she was doing.

Once we got to the Outcome Frame and resolved their conflict, Greg, Grace, and Caroline all had insights about turning their differences into strengths. All three saw what they lost because they were stuck in the Blame Frame—not only the client, but also their trust in each other. Greg realized he could have had a lot of help from Grace and Caroline if he had been open to receiving it. Grace and Caroline understood what they could do in similar situations in the future.

Answers are things we use to solidify our own position. Don't look for answers, look for insight.

"Ah-hah" Moments

I tell all my workshop participants not to look for answers. Answers are things we use to solidify our own positions. Instead, look for insights. Insights mean we're learning something. Insights mean we're filling that hole in our minds that I call what-we-don't-know-we-don't-know.

In all the conflicts I describe in this chapter, I was there to coach the participants toward resolution. But how can you switch from Blame Frame to Outcome Frame on your own? In the world we live and work in, it's easy to fall into Blame Frame. It's easy to react to a conflict by pointing a finger. Shifting to Outcome Frame requires some self-discipline. Conflicts are very private. Many conflicts take place inside people's heads. Often there is no confrontation at all. So you have to shift to Outcome Frame on your own, which also requires a certain amount of determination.

Here's what you can do to work out whether you're in Blame Frame or Outcome Frame. Think of a recent cross-gender conflict. Describe what you did. What frame of reference did you use? Blame or Outcome? To find out, answer the following:

Did you

❏   Decide the other person was wrong?

❏   Argue about who was right or wrong?

❏   Say, "I'm not responsible for this!"

❏   Walk away in anger or shock?

❏   Gossip?

❏ Keep mulling it over?

❏ Get defensive?

❏ Feel victimized, wrongly accused, misunderstood, or misinterpreted?

❏ Feel invalidated?

If you answered "Yes" to most of these questions, you're in the Blame Frame.

Or, did you *Tips to outcome frame.*

❏ Stand back and reflect?

❏ Decide you were committed to this relationship?

❏ Take responsibility for dealing with the conflict?

❏ Take proactive steps toward finding a solution?

❏ Try to look for a win-win solution?

If you answered "Yes" to most of these questions, congratulations! You are in the Outcome Frame.

Here are three simple steps to help you get to a win-win solution:

1. **Co-create a win-win solution.**
   Affirm your mutual understanding; make sure you both feel heard and understood. You could start by saying, "You may not have meant anything by this, but…" or, "I need to clarify something." This is the hardest part for both men and women: to stay with the conversation until it's complete. Aim for a clean slate. Brainstorm together for multiple win-win solutions for the future. Concentrate on steps 2 and 3, and keep your word.

2. **Frame the conversation.**
   Identify the goal: "I have a conflict, and I'm here to see a win-win solution," or, "There's something I need to resolve with you." Establish that your immediate goal is mutual understanding.

3. **Check in.**
   Ask for each other's help toward this understanding. Do not defend or disagree or you will fall back into the Blame Frame. Seek to understand before being understood. Repeat the other

person's position in your own words: "I may have made an assumption, but…" or, "I may have misinterpreted, but…."

Women, don't forget: there's nothing that frustrates men more than feeling that they are the problem instead of part of the solution. And men: there's nothing that frustrates women more than "not being heard" and understood.

Conflict resolution is a tool we can use once a misunderstanding has occurred. My hope and intention is that it is a tool we will require less frequently as our gender intelligence improves.

I started this book as a conversation about gender difference. Now I encourage you to carry on that conversation. Take any chapter of this book and use it to start a discussion among your coworkers. Whether it's to talk about the challenges of working with the opposite gender, or about how you interpret words and actions differently, every chapter in this book can be used to start investigating gender difference in a non-blaming way. Every topic discussed can be used to help you and your coworkers move from a denying to a tolerant attitude toward differences, and with such an attitude shift, you will see clearly how understanding gender differences can be beneficial to everyone.

Afterword

One of the most crucial steps in business today is the system seeing itself.

—Peter M. Senge, author of *The Fifth Discipline*

Imagine a critical mass of men and women who truly collaborate. It would consist of men who could see as women see and of women who could see as men see. Then the women would be able to speak for the men, and the men would be able to speak for the women. More to the point, each man and woman could speak as a unique individual, bringing to the table his or her particular vision, creativity, and thinking. It would be the end of "groupthink," and it would be the start of an inclusive culture in which people would really put their heads together to solve a problem or achieve a goal.

It would be a win-win for whichever organization got there first with such a culture. And it just might save the world, too.

—*Barbara Annis*

Further Reading

Amen, Daniel G. *Change Your Brain, Change Your Life: The Breakthrough Program for Conquering Anxiety, Depression, Obsessiveness, Anger, and Impulsiveness.* New York: Three River Press, 1999.

Andreae, Simon. *Anatomy of Desire: The Science and Psychology of Sex, Love and Marriage.* London: Little, Brown and Company, 1998.

Arburdene, Patricia, and John Naisbitt. *Megatrends for Women: From Liberation to Leadership.* London: Arrow, 1994.

Archer, John, and Barbara Lloyd. *Sex and Gender.* Cambridge: Cambridge University Press, 1995.

Bloom, Howard. *Global Brain: The Evolution of Mass Mind from the Big Bang to the 21st Century.* New York: John Wiley & Sons, 2001.

Blum, Deborah. *Sex on the Brain: The Biological Differences between Men and Women.* New York: Penguin Books, 1998.

Burr, Chandler I. *A Separate Creation.* London: Bantam Press, 1997.

Canary, Daniel J., and Tara M. Emmers-Sommer. *Sex and Gender Differences in Personal Relationships.* New York: The Guilford Press, 1998.

Carper, Jean. *Your Miracle Brain.* New York: HarperCollins Publishers, 2001.

Coates, Jennifer. *Women, Men and Language.* Longman, 1993.

Covey, Stephen R. *The 7 Habits of Highly Effective People: Powerful Lessons in Personal Change*. Simon & Schuster, 2002.

Eisler, Riane. *The Chalice & the Blade: Our History, Our Future*. Peter Smith Publishing, 1994.

Eisler, Riane. *The Partnership Way: New Tools for Living and Learning, Healing Our Families, and Our World*. New World Library, 2002.

Fisher, Helen. *The First Sex: The Natural Talents of Women and How They Are Changing the World*. New York: Ballantine Publishing Group, 1999.

Gardner, Howard. *Extraordinary Minds*. London: Phoenix, 1998.

Gilligan, Carol. *In a Different Voice: Psychological Theory and Women's Development*. Cambridge, MA: Harvard University Press, 1982.

Gray, John. *Men, Women and Relationships: Making Peace with the Opposite Sex*. Beyond Words, 1993.

Heim, Pat and Susan Murphy. *In the Company of Women*. New York: Penguin Putnam, 2001.

Helgesen, Sally. *The Female Advantage: Women's Way of Leadership*. New York: Doubleday, 1995.

Hendrix, Harville. *Getting the Love You Want: A Guide for Couples*. Pocket Books, 1993.

Humphrey, Nicholas. *A History of the Mind*. Vintage, 1993.

Jaworski, Joseph. *Synchronicity: The Inner Path of Leadership*. San Francisco: Berrett-Koehler Publishers, Inc., 1996.

Jensen, Eric. *Brain-Based Learning: The New Paradigm of Teaching*. Turning Point Publications, 1995.

Maccoby, Eleanor and Carol Nagy Jacklin. *The Psychology of Sex Differences*. Palo Alto, CA: Stanford University Press, 1974.

Markova, Dawn. *Open Mind: Exploring the 6 Patterns of Natural Intelligence*. Conari Press, 1997.

McGraw, Phillip. *Self Matters: Creating Your Life from the Inside Out*. New York: Simon & Schuster, 2002.

Moir, Anne, and David Jessel. *Brain Sex: The Real Difference between Men and Women*. Mandarin, 1991.

Ong, Walter J. *Fighting for Life: Contest, Sexuality and Consciousness*. Ithaca, NY: Cornell University Press, 1981.

Pinker, Steven. *The Blank Slate: The Modern Denial of Human Nature*. New York: Penguin Books, 2002.

Popcorn, Faith. *Evolution: Understanding Women*. Hyperion, 2000.

Reisner, Paul. *Couplehood*. New York: Bantam Press, 1994.

Saint-Onge, Hubert and Debra Wallace. *Leveraging Communities of Practice for Strategic Advantage*. Butterworth-Heinemann, 2002.

Senge, Peter. *The Dance of Change: The Challenges of Sustaining Momentum in Learning Organizations*. New York: Doubleday, 1999.

Stone, Douglas, Bruce Patton, and Sheila Heen. *Difficult Conversations: How to Discuss What Matters Most*. New York: Penguin Books, 1999.

Tannen, Deborah. *The Argument Culture: Stopping America's War of Words*. Ballantine Books, 1999.

Tannen, Deborah. *That's Not What I Meant!: How Conversational Style Makes or Breaks Relationships*. Virago Press, 1992.

Tannen, Deborah. *You Just Don't Understand: Women and Men in Conversation*. Virago Press, 1990.

Yaccato, Joanne Thomas. *The 80% Minority*. Penguin, 2003.

Index